Mary O'Donnell

John Healy

nineteen
acres

NINETEEN ACRES

© John Healy 1978

ISBN 0 9512639 0 0

First published 1978 by Kenny's Bookshop & Art Galleries Ltd., Galway.

This edition published 1987 by the House of Healy, Achill.

Typeset and printed by the Leinster Leader Ltd., Naas, Co. Kildare.

For Evelyn

NORA O'DONNELL

(FOR JOHN HEALY)

Nora O'Donnell knows how not to die.
This is the steel achievement of blood.
I see her coming out of hospital
Pausing a moment at the side of the road
Where the first house stood.
                              The first house.
The first garden. The first woman. Nora O'Donnell,
There's work to do, death must be put in its place,
This is acceptable and not without honour.
She is a small town, a fire, Botuney Bridge, a bed
Where love is made in the silence it deserves
And you are born to say whatever is in you to say,
Angered by the living, enlightened by the dead,
Knowing the half-hearted thing is what is killing us.
Let the robin sing its heart out in the bush today.

BRENDAN KENNELLY

FOREWORD

There is one special book in every man and woman if they had the time, courage, sense, vision and detachment to write it. I would call that book a book of human, personal truth because it would be based on the suffered and enjoyed facts of the writer's life. Hewn out of personal experience, it would delight readers in that special way that moves the heart and mind when one is drinking from the bittersweet cup of truth. John Healy's *Nineteen Acres* is such a book. There isn't a false note in it because Healy knew everything about his world and his people before he put pen to paper.

But what *is* the *Nineteen Acres*? To begin with, there is the truth of a vital portion of one man's life, told in candid, accurate language. John Healy is a superb journalist: he writes with curiosity, eloquence, humour, compassion, savagery, and a clinical, incisive power of analysis that suggests both the surgeon's knife and the healing touch. He writes to understand difficult, tangled matters and people; his genius as a journalist is that he can unravel all that difficulty and communicate it to others with clarity and force. That clarity and force are present all through *Nineteen Acres*, especially in the way Healy recognises and expresses his fierce, steady, boyish resolution to become a journalist, his sense of the dignity and responsibility of that way of life, and his determination to excel at no matter what cost to himself. That dream of excellence is at the heart of this book; it is inspiringly described.

So much for the individual dream. *Nineteen Acres* is also a picture of family life and of the family in the larger community. The joys, sorrows, tasks, tempers, talks, the sheer implacable *dailiness* of living, the boy in the family, the family in the community, the community reflecting the fortunes and misfortunes of the nation – all this is presented with instinctive authority and precision. I hesitate to call it a social document because that might imply, to some, an absence of imaginative power; but *Nineteen Acres* is both vigorous social history and imaginative creation.

I've heard the distinguished Abbey actor, Peadar Lambe, read this book on RTÉ Radio. I found it a deeply moving experience. Lambe's voice brought out all the subtleties of the dialogue and of the narrative prose, all the moments of tension and revelation in this deep-cutting but always lucid work. *Nineteen Acres* will be read a long time from now by people yet unborn; and I know full well they will enjoy it as much as I did because they too will be riveted by this story of the truth of one man's life told in a way that cannot fail to enrich the lives of all those fortunate enough to read it.

BRENDAN KENNELLY

CHAPTER ONE

It isn't much of a road and it doesn't lead to much of a holding. The road is clay-topped and rutted. The holding is just over nineteen acres. Half of it is reclaimed bog. The other hilly half, above the house on the hill, is lean and rock-ribbed. The house is red tiled, with a thick shelter belt of pines to cut the east wind. Behind it, older and better-spaced pines and ash trees, which made a shelter belt for the old thatched house, now stand gap-toothed.

Now, once again, the black hearse stops on the tar road, where it joins the dirt road.

It is a long minute . . .

Few people in the long cortège behind knew the history of that spot where the hearse had stopped. It was the parting place of the O'Donnells.

Down this rutted road, from the thatched cottage on the hill, Jamesie O'Donnell and Mary O'Donnell brought the fruit of their marriage bed, one after another, until there was only one left, and sent them out into the world to do their best.

When they met the tar road, Mary O'Donnell would kiss son or daughter good-bye. The girls were the first to go.

It was on this spot she parted with her first daughter Mary. The farewell was short and simple. Mary was bound for America and Brooklyn. Her mother was happy she was going to kinfolk. She would be all right.

"Keep your mouth and your legs closed. Keep your ears open. And send home the ticket for Anna."

And as Jamesie O'Donnell drove young Mary O'Donnell into the

1

town of Charlestown to take the train to Queenstown and the ship to America, there was only the sound of the harness and the pony's steady trot under the trap to make conversation.

Jamesie O'Donnell, like many strong men, had few words at a time like this.

His wife, now walking back up the road to the thatched cottage, could be a mother again. No one would see her tears and her face would be dried in the shower-of-hailstones apron before she climbed the hill to the house and the rest of her children. Five times in the opening decade of the twentieth century Jamesie O'Donnell and his wife Mary, came this road to part at the tar.

For young Mary, the daughter, sent home the ticket for her sister, Anna.

Anna, in her turn, sent the ticket home for Nora. Nora sent it home for Kit.

It was with Kit's going that the ritual farewell was changed. "Keep your mouth and your legs closed. Keep your ears open – an' between ye, let ye send home the slates."

One son, Michael, came down this road with England as his destination.

Jim alone stayed.

They had gone their way in innocence and wonder. No one knew then that the rich seed of that holding would, in their innocence, be plunged into the world's biggest disasters. They came straight from a thatched rural cottage in the West of Ireland, to become front line soldiers in two of the world's great dramas, the First World War which took the lives of millions and, more lethal still in its devastation, the greater disaster which followed on the Armistice of Peace: the dreaded flu known as the Spanish Lady which was to claim over 21,000,000 lives in the 120 black and agonising days that epidemic lasted.

Anna O'Donnell was a nurse. She never came back. The flu she had fought in others in the frightened city of Brooklyn claimed her.

Michael O'Donnell never came back. He grew up hearing his father read for his neighbours the speeches from *Hansard* of old John

Dillon. Jamesie O'Donnell had followed Michael Davitt and his Land Leaguers from Straide, for the cause of the land was sacred: the Old Irish Parliamentary Party men were not distant people under that thatch, for Jamesie O'Donnell put his heart into his reading for his neighbours and he had a pride of his own in delivering the speeches of the Irish leaders in the House of Commons. So that when Captain Redmond called for patriotic Irishmen to join the Volunteers, young Michael O'Donnell went down the road first to shoulder a pick and shovel and later to shoulder his English gun, sure in the knowledge he was fighting Ireland's cause.

He was wounded in France, and when Ireland fought its own battle to leave the Empire and the Irish Parliamentary Party was wiped out, and Redmond's Volunteers portrayed as traitors, he learned not to be in any hurry home. We would see his two sons evacuated from wartime England in the Second World War but I would not see Michael when his father and mother were themselves brought down this road for the last time to their graves in Carracastle, in the Nineteen Forties.

Jim would be there, for Jim, who had stayed at home, followed de Valera, did what he had to do in The Movement, and made little of it. He would fight the Economic War and do what de Valera said had to be done and make little of it.

Mary survived the flu to marry and produce one son who'd die before her. She would die on the poverty line in New York and would leave her dust in America.

Kit, the third of three nurses this holding gave to New York, would survive, too, and, on the dockside, snatch the attractive widower who was on his way back to Ireland to marry her sister Nora.

Nora O'Donnell survived the flu, kept her mouth and her legs closed, kept her ears open and kept this holding in her mind's eye. She it was who came home and brought the slates with her and, with the others, had kept the holding stocked and tided Jamesie and Mary O'Donnell and her brother Jim, over the worst of the Economic War. She would see Jim marry and bring Mary Anne MacManus from Barroe into the new house. As the new district midwife she would attend Mary Anne and when Mary Anne failed to produce a child

3

("there was no child there ever – it was the bloody change was on her: she was too old for our Jim") she would assume a moral ascendancy over her, for Nora produced five.

It would be later, with the arrival of Michael's two nephews, evacuees home from England, that she would begin to fear about the holding and who would get it. For if Jim was without issue, he might leave it to Michael's two sons. That threat passed with their leaving after the war but by now the holding and its memories – the things which sustained her in New York in the fearful days of the world's flu epidemic, how hard she worked, how much she had sent home – would obsess her.

She feared Jim O'Donnell's sudden death: It would leave the land in the hands of Mary Anne from the next village where "the long-tailed crowd from Barroe" were, as she imagined, sitting and waiting to walk into the great holding on Castleduff hillside.

She herself would be widowed. She would come this same road with her own daughter. She would spend two hours on an operating table where Ireland's finest doctors would give her less than a fifty-fifty chance, for she was seventy. She would perplex them with her resilience but they did not know she had vowed to outlive Mary Anne and see the holding stay with the seed of the O'Donnells.

She had worked and fought and loved and hated and cajoled and coaxed and lived for the day a son of her's would have this holding and be proud of it. Until that day came, she would not die . . .

That August day in 1972, we looked up the length of the dust-road. The red tiles gleamed. The shelter belt thrived. The fields were green: there was sap in them. The other houses on that stretch of hillside where she had neighbours were empty. The very fields looked listless and neglected. O'Donnells alone it seemed, had the vitality and the holding looked snug and comfortable. The seed from it had a prodigal scattering over two continents and three countries. They were all gone now, making generous dust in the graves of three nations. Nora was the last of them . . .

The hearse moved on again. It was only three-quarters of a mile to Carracastle graveyard where Nora O'Donnell, well satisfied, would lie

4

easy at last, with her husband, her dead daughter and her unborn child, her father and mother, her brother and her sister-in-law.

I needed no one to tell me that Nora O'Donnell was the last of a great generation of a great, if anonymous, people who lived and loved and sweated and laughed and cried and worked again on and over this now economist-despised holding of nineteen acres.

Nora O'Donnell was my mother.

CHAPTER TWO

Nora O'Donnell was born and reared under the golden thatch. It was a long, low house, with its front facing north, looking out over the long valley which was mostly brown bog running away to the blue of the Ox Mountains; it was a scene painted in the colours of Frank McKelvey in his prime. To the west, Nephin Mountain stood guard in the evening sunset. To the east there was nothing but the cold wind. South, behind the house, there was the apple orchard. The Top Fields started to rise behind that and kept on rising until the land ended on the top of Mullaghanoe Mountain which, in truth, was but a gentle hill. Between Castleduff and Mullaghanoe there was the Top Village. It had a name but it was always the Top Village.

The house was on the brow of the hill. It was on firm dry ground for later they would open the face of the hill for sand and gravel. Directly beneath it ran a dirt road and there the bogland started. The dirt road, winter or summer, was always wet, for two or three spring wells never dried up.

The Bottom Meadow, always thick and heavy of swarth, ran under the hill. It was long and narrow: it had been reclaimed from the bog by Grandda. It was to be kept sweet through three generations. On the mearing still untamed, the bog held sway. It still holds sway but for an odd handkerchief-sized patch of grass. Further down the dirt road, towards the tar road, was The Big Meadow. It, too, had been reclaimed with the loy and here Jamesie O'Donnell sowed his Aran Banners ("Bog Banners") on one strip, with a couple of hundred of Early York cabbage plants stuck in the side of the ridges so that the ground earned its keep twice. In the late summer you could see the

6

potato stalks browning, the big heads of cabbage green, the hay cocked golden brown and clamps of black turf all in this one busy field.

The top fields were kept for grazing but had been sub-divided too. Behind the house the land was ribbed with rocks which came through the thin soil like the ribs of a fodder-starved, in-calf heifer. The far end of the Top Field was ploughed for oats or potatoes. Champions, Kerr's Pinks or Records mightn't crop as big as the Bog Banners but these were table potatoes for the house and for seed and, in the spring of the year, for the market within in Charlestown.

They were balls of flour coming off that dry stony soil. The crops would rotate between potatoes and oats. The oats went for the chickens, turkeys and geese, a mash for the horse, some for seed and, again, some for the market-day in Charlestown. The shed was to the east and was open.

In the haggard, Grandma had a small vegetable patch and it was here they sowed the May Queens for the first new spuds of the year, the Earlies. Here she grew "the greens', as she called the early cabbage.

When I first went to live there for the summer, there were three rooms in the house. The front was whitewashed each year, always before the rose bushes started to send out the shoots which, later, would produce a profusion of big heavily-scented cabbage roses. They went right up to the thatch.

The kitchen was small and clean.

Inside the door St. Patrick, in regal green, sternly banished the snakes from Ireland. On the other side, bould Robert Emmet remained always in that half-Napoleonic stance, declaiming silently his determination to banish the Sassenach snakes from this same land.

On the small window, *Old Moore's Almanac* hung from a nail. Behind you was the dresser as part of the back wall. Off the fire was the cailleach[1] bed, with a long form in front of it. It could be used to sit at the fire or to seat us at the plain deal table, which was scrubbed three times a day so that the knots now stood out over the grain.

1. Bed by the kitchen fire.

The turf fire burned best at night. In the day it was a functional thing, for pots had to be boiled for the pigs, for the dinner, for the hens, and bread had to be baked: It had to be fed from the ciseán[2] of sally rods. No sooner would the sods start to glow but they had to be clothed again with more of the long black Glosh sods of turf. The lid of the iron kettle always seemed to be hopping, a daytime cricket gone mad.

It was in this house my mother was born. She grew up, as I was to grow up later, in this warm kitchen. She knew the busy working fire and knew the relaxed fire at the end of the day when, after tea and the milking, Grandma would pull out the griosach[3] – the coals and ash of the busy day-fires – to the front of the hearth, stand fresh sods to the back, rebuild the heart of the fire with the coals of the day and then sit, content, to listen as Grandda milked the cows.

From this kitchen you could hear the lowing cattle and the rich sound as the milking went on. Grandma had scalded the buckets. The first cow might be nervous. She'd be a kicker. She'd get a thump.

"Stand up there to hell with ye" and the first streams hit the bucket with a metallic sound. Soon the sound grew richer and deeper as the bucket filled.

Now the puseens,[4] mewling at the door of the cowhouse, could be heard in the calm of the evening. A mile away the dogs barked. Across the hill, at McGloin's, young calves nosed and licked their way into buckets of milk and mash and the sound, as the buckets hit the iron gates, went the length of the village. The cats would be fed, the horse foddered and in the dusk now there'd be a stillness.

Over the bog, in the thin blue air, the minaun aerach[5] climbed into the sky with the mating call, giota-giota-giota, until, at the top of the flight, he'd plummet to the earth, his tail feathers spread so that the air rushed through them to make the evening cry of the drumming snipe in love. The days were long and busy, even for a child. The child ran the messages.

2. Basket.
3. Glowing fire embers.
4. Kittens.
5. Snipe.

"Run down to the well, agradh,[6] for a can of water." Or: "Run out, agradh, for a breast of turf." Or: "Run down, agradh, and tell the men to come up to the dinner" (this if they were cutting the Bottom Meadow, or the Bog Meadow). When Grandma had strained the milk into the cream crocks, scalded the straining muslin and put it out on the hedge for the night, the last of her day ended.

Now we sat at the glowing fire. Grandda sat direclty in front on a chair. He said little. Slowly, his gaze deep in the fire, he would circle one thumb with another and his right foot would keep time to some tuneless air he never sang.

Grandma, sitting as near as she could to the oil lamp, would have a thick woollen sock pulled up on the back of her wrist and the needle would work away to patch the hole on the heel of it. There would be only three noises. The three big cats purring contented and, as if mimicking Grandda, they, too, gazed deep into the red coals. You felt that they had been there centuries ago and had spent this hour alert and wide-eyed at the dawn of time, waiting for sight of the first crickets ever to sing from the hidden hearth and, though now they knew they would not ever see them and had to be content with the sound, they could not throw off the enigmatic watchfulness. Now the cricket song broke the slow measured tick-and-stop-and-tock of the brown-faced clock over the mantlepiece.

There was no need for words now. The clock would strike ten. Grandma would put her sewing aside. From a nail on the wall she'd take the big Rosary beads and, without anything more than her ritual, "Let ye get down on yer knees and we'll say the Rosary in the name of God", we got up from our seats, knelt down with our backs to the fire and one another, leaned our elbows on the seat or the form, and made the responses.

It was so in my mother's day and it would be so in my childhood days, whether in Castleduff or in my own home in Charlestown.

Grandma had her own trimmings and they were as long again as the Rosary. But it was from the trimmings that I learned there was another world and another family bigger than the gathering in this

6. Love.

9

kitchen. She prayed for her father and mother. She prayed for Grandda's father and mother. She prayed for Anna who had died in America. She prayed for Mary Flaherty and her son, John. She prayed for Mary's dead husband. She prayed for Kit and Pat O'Neill. She prayed for the bit of good weather to get The Bottom Meadow. She prayed for her son Michael. And then she prayed for all the poor souls "in purgatory this night" that "God will be good to them in the end of all".

Looking back now, I think Grandda used to find it kind of hard and towards the end of that sonorous recital, he'd give the chair a push across the floor as if to say: "You have prayed enough, woman."

It didn't worry Grandma. If she wanted to say three Hail Marys that the Bog Banners, due to be dug next week, would crop well, she said them and all the scraping that Grandda or Uncle Jim did with their chairs wasn't going to put her off.

She used to pray for Nora. "Three Hail Marys that God may send Nora luck next month."

I didn't know then who Nora was and I didn't know what kind of luck Nora wanted. Nora sounded as much a stranger to me as was dead Anna, absent Michael, Kit and Pat O'Neill and John and Mary Flaherty. But I do remember it was more than a coincidence that when Grandma prayed hardest that God would send Nora luck next month or next week, I would go home at the end of the summer to find a new baby in our house in Charlestown. It took me a few summers to realise that "Nora" and my mother were one person.

There was no radio then: television, with its instant world, was decades in the future.

But when Grandma got on her knees each night for the Rosary, she shrank the world with her beads. Her three Hail Marys linked the black polly heifer and her welfare with that of her daughters, Kit and Mary in far New York, and back again to her son Michael in England; Michael might be a political outcast because he followed Redmond but he was still her son at Rosary time.

The fire was raked, the ashes of the day thrown up on the coals of the night, five or six sods thrown on top of that and then it was bedtime on feather beds. One day was ended and one night was ahead but the fire would be the link between today and tomorrow, between this week and next, between one year and another and whatever happened it would not go out. They would build a slated house and quench the old hearth but the quenching would not be done before the new fire built of the coals from the old hearth across the street, was safely glowing. The fire was life and continuity. The old day died in its rakings and the new day began in its kindlings, but, like the gentle heartbeat of the sleeping people, the heart of the fire itself maintained the continuity from dark to dawn and from dawn to dark again. In the end it would be this same fire and its power which would confront me in one of the most agonising moments of my life . . .

CHAPTER THREE

Living in this house in those long-gone summers of the 'Thirties gave me a good idea of how my mother, as a young girl, had grown up here. Nothing had changed much. The top room where the girls had slept, and the boys with them, was now the dairy. Grandma kept her bowls of milk there to thicken for the churning. She had a dash churn and her row of wooden bowls and squares of muslin. On churning day she'd scald everything with iron kettles of hot water. I would run to the well several times that day and the last can of water went for the washing up afterwards, when everything had been scalded again.

The rhythm was even and fixed: the wants were small and if you didn't have it, you went without. In those days you wanted for little enough on small holdings like those.

Four times a day the big pot went on with the Bog Banners for the pigs and chickens. On top of every pot Grandma would have the potheens,[7] the small spuds she'd pick from the eating potatoes above in the dairy.

They'd be for bruisey for John Joe, for she always gave me my two names (as indeed did the rest of the village). Bruisey is mashed potatoes creamed with country butter and a drop of milk. "Eat that and you'll grow to a man", she'd say, as she mashed and mixed with a fork.

The midday meal came off the holding. Cabbage boiled with a lump of fat bacon from the pig Jim killed each spring and autumn was "a great tightner", washed down with fresh buttermilk with some crumbs of ungathered butter still floating on the top.

7. Small potatoes.

Jim O'Donnell was a hearty eater. He'd take the pot of Champions, boiling on the crook, and throw them into the sally rod cisean in clouds of steam: I can still smell the spuds and wet rods today. He'd lump the cracked spuds on a tray on the centre of the table, with Grandma putting down the plates with the cabbage and shivering bacon. Jim's grace-before-meals was short and sweet: "Come on – let ye have at it. Eat up there, young fellow." It didn't matter that the young fellow had a feed of bruisey only an hour before, you had to eat up. "That'll put hair on your chest", Jim would say. I wasn't sure I wanted hair on my chest.

At the end, Jim would push back his chair, stretch his corduroyed legs, open the big brass buckled belt and let his stomach expand. That was a "tightner". A "stiffner" was something else. When the first of the May Queens were dug, Grandma made cally. You scraped the light skins off the new potatoes, pot-boiled them and then, with a pounder, pounded them into mash, mixing in salt and chopped scallions and some fresh milk. You piled it on the plates like a white castle, scooped out the centre and into it you put a dollop of fresh butter. When it became molten gold in the heart of the castle, you started on the outside, scraped the walls of the castle, dunked what you had gathered into the well of butter and ate it. Inevitably the walls were eaten away and when the liquid butter broke through the walls, you plunged your spoon in, mixed up the lot and polished it off.

The mug of buttermilk was your dessert.

Now, one day, old Charlie Ward, the tinker man, came stalking the street past the kitchen window and we had just about finished the first cally of the year. We were hay-making in the Bottom Meadow and Uncle Jim, who never missed a chance for a practical joke, saw Charlie coming to the back door.

"The devil mend him", he said to himself and then, as soon as Charlie, from the door, blessed all here and spared us God's health and blessings, Jim shouted: "Come up to the table, Charlie. You'll have something to ate, for I'm thinking 'tis a long step you had on this hot day out from the town."

Charlie, taking the cap off his hang-dog head, agreed "it was surely." He sat down.

"Here, woman, you'll give this man something to ate." When Grandma came with the plate of cally, Jim took it off her.

"Sure, where would you be going with that biteen for a man as big as Big Charlie: here, give it to me", said Jim, taking the plate from her. He heaped it to the edges and put it down before Charlie. "Oh an' the blessin's of God on you an' all here but ye're too kind altogether."

If he knew Jim O'Donnell he'd have been a bit more sparing on his prayers! Jim, the devilment dancing already in his eyes, watched poor Charlie wolfing it into him.

"Here", said Jim, pushing the jug of buttermilk over to Charlie, "wet your whistle with that, Charlie."

For half an hour we sat, Grandma throwing a wary eye at Jim while Charlie stuffed himself with cally and buttermilk. When he finished the plate, Jim went back and scraped the pot. Charlie protested he had enough.

"Here, damn you to hell – you'll finish it: you can work it off in the meadow below for I think it'll be a good evening for hay-making."

Charlie, with less enthusiasm now, ate up. The jug was passed again, refilled from the sweet can of buttermilk on the side-dresser.

"Wire into it, Charlie – God knows when we'll be ating again." The poor fellow couldn't finish. By now Jim had got his rest and his stretch and he went out to the hayshed and got a fork for Charlie. "Right, Charlie, you'll shake out for the evening after a feed like that. Come on."

Charlie got up. He hinted he wasn't much in a hay-field. "There'll be no loss on you – we're shaking out." We went down. I carried the can of drink: a mixture of spring water and milk, laced with oaten meal – a great thirst quencher in a meadow. It was only when we had a meitheal[8] you brought porter in the sweet can.

The meadow was cut the day before and the grass lay in swarths.

8. Group sharing work.

14

Each man took a swarth and shook out the grass loosely. Youngsters like me used our hands, for the forks were often taller than us and made it too awkward. (If a fork had been broken in mid-handle the year before, you could have it: if not, the hands did the job and you had to take your chances if there were thistles in the grass to spike your fingers.)

Jim put Charlie on the first swarth and he took the second. "Right, Charlie, shake it out." For five minutes the sweat rolled off Charlie Ward.

Between Jim behind him, damning and blasting him on, the sun overhead blistering him, an odd jab of the fork from Jim, but worst of all the fermenting mixture of buttermilk and cally, the poor man was sweating like a bull. The more he slowed down, the more Jim appeared to drive him on. "What the hell is wrong with you, Charlie, after the fine tightner of cally you had", Jim asked with mock incredulity. In the end it was too much for Charlie: he had to go by the stone fence to lie down and sleep it off.

"Well, the devil mend ye", said Jim, smiling, taking a swig of the oaten drink.

Charlie, in truth, had a "stiffener": he had eaten and drunk so much that he couldn't stir, never mind make hay.

When, two hours later, Charlie got up like a man who had a bad hangover, Jim told him he was no bloody use in a hay-field and he'd make him two ponnies – tin mugs – and bring them the next time he came the way.

"An' I will surely, Mister O'Donnell, and the blessings of God and His Holy Mother on you and yours."

He was as good as his word. When he came again he had two ponnies with handles on them and a quart measure made, like the ponnies, out of gleaming tin, for Grandma.

At four in the evening the sweet can of tea came to the meadow, sugared and milked and golden. The bouquet of that tea, when you lifted the lid off it, is still with me.

So, too, is the smell of the freshly-baked bread, so hot that the lump of fresh butter soaked into it. The tea over, it was time for me to

15

tackle up the ass and cart for Grandda. We had to bring the cans of fresh milk down to the cross-roads at Carracastle for "the creamery". You never saw the creamery man: you just left the milkcans at the cross and picked up the set of milkcans left there with the skimmed milk.

Grandda would lug them up on the back of the cart, give me the reins for the return journey and, with his feet dangling over the shaft, and mine dangling on the other side, we'd set off for home. For now that you were allowed to drive an ass and cart you would surely reach manhood when, some day, Jim would let you drive Dolly and the big horse-cart. Or, better still, give you the reins going down to Mass in the trap on a Sunday morning.

These were the years of the Economic War. I knew nothing about it then. True, in Charlestown I would see the hundreds of bicycles come down from all the townlands around Charlestown for the "free beef". You'd see the men wobbling home, parcels of fresh meat under the springs of the carriers, the blood coming through the brown paper.

Years afterwards, reading of those times, I could not recognise them from the life on the hill in Castleduff. It may be the "mix" (as the jargon boys of the Nineteen Seventies call it now) and the cheques from America which saw Jim comfortably through those times. The skim milk we brought home from the cross-roads would go to the pigs and the bonhams or, when we had them, to the suck calves. The meadows were good even if they were bog meadows: the hay-shed would be full and there'd be two or three ricks over in the haggard. There'd be a good threshing of straw for bedding. There'd be turnips from the Bog Meadow and pits of Bog Banners for the winter and spring.

There would be chickens for the Sunday dinner table and, if someone was sick, the chicken would be killed for broth and the white flesh fed to the invalid. There was no want in this house in those days. The creamery cheque was coming in. The shop bills were paid in spring and autumn when Jim "sold". It might be a cartload of bonhams in the fair of Charlestown or a pair of bullocks or heifers on the Square of Charlestown. The suits of clothes came from America, always navy blue

16

and always camphored. Shirts and shoes came the same way and Grandma was handy with the needle, to let out or take in. On Sunday morning Jim was immaculate in navy blue, a thin gold chain across his ample waist-coated front when he went to Mass. Grandma took down her astrakhan coat, still as camphored as it came, and her black heavy hat with the spotted veil. She was small but she was elegant in Sunday morning clothes.

After Mass, Grandda and Jim might slip away to Davey's pub for a quick drink: Grandma would keep me with her talking to the neighbours. A public house was no place for a woman or a child. Anyway, this was the one hour or two of the week she ever left the house or had time to talk to her busy neighbours. If they had a can of sweets or Rainbow Caramels, Jim would have a pennorth of them when he came back to the horse and trap to drive us home. There, he'd take off the navy suit and the good shoes, get into his "duds", as he called his week-day clothes, and get on with the chores of the morning.

On Sunday evening, when we moved to the new house, he'd take out the old gramophone my mother had brought home from New York with her and, cranking it up after he had tested the needle, he'd play the "phonograph records", as he called them. They were all from America: jigs, reels, and hornpipes by Coleman from Killavil who had "done well for himself in America". He was good, but he was never as good as Michael Freeman of Lisacul, for he was one of our own, a relation on Grandma's side.

And we had the nonsense songs like "Me ould Skillara Hat". Grandda would sit, as grave as if he were in the presence of some great symphony orchestra, the thumbs caressing each other and he would have little to say.

Grandma never sat still, for she'd be beetling round the kitchen inventing jobs for herself. She'd have potato cakes to make if there were any potatoes over from the lunch. If it was a cock had been killed for the Sunday dinner and there were "pickings" on him, she'd put them on plates: if not, the eggs would be boiled, one each, and two for Jim and, as an especial treat, shop jam would be put on a saucer and the jam-jar put away for another week and another Sunday.

The fresh soda cake she'd slice against her chest until the plate was full. Later, she'd make "gruelly" for the supper: a skillet pot of oaten meal, thick to the point where you could cut it in sections from the pot when it cooled.

In the old days, when she was young and some of her people first set sail for America, they'd be baking cakes of "gruelly" for days beforehand, for it was one of the few things, like the oaten cake, which kept on a long voyage at a time when you had to travel "steerage" and fend for yourself. Mary had to bring the oaten "gruelly" and the oaten cake, though conditions had changed enough for her to be able to dispense with both. Grandma had been told that the ships were now feeding the people too, but the tradition was deep in her. How did she know but it was all a pack of lies so that you'd go without your provisions and have to buy them on the ship when you might want all your money for something else, agradh?

It was a precaution like many other precautions which the old people of Grandma's day believed in, for they had heard many a harrowing story of the Famine crossings. The sharks who had preyed on the shoals of poor Irish emigrants in the Eighteen Forties, Fifties and Sixties – when they had been forced, by trade, to travel to Liverpool to catch the ship to America – lived on in the folk memory. They had been swindled out of what little money they had by sharpies on the waterfront or by unscrupulous crew men.

The night before Mary went – as I would learn in Brooklyn many years later – Grandma had spent sewing ten sovereigns and fifteen pounds in paper money into the lining of her overcoat. "And always wear it until you get there, agradh."

And Mary had never left it off her, night or day, until she reached Brooklyn. A year after she arrived and was settled in a job as a kitchen maid, she made up her first clothes parcel and sent it home. In the coat for Grandma, sewed as Grandma had sewed them, were the gold sovereigns, for, as she explained, "Anna would want them when it was her turn to come." The same gold sovereigns crossed and recrossed the Atlantic four times and when the last had gone they came back again to Castleduff to soften what hard times were in

18

Ireland then. It may have been some of those same sovereigns which tided Grandma and Grandda over the 'thirties . I have more than a suspicion most of them went when Grandma's first and only daughter to marry out of Castleduff came to wed Stephen Healy within in the town of Charlestown . . .

CHAPTER FOUR

My mother married Stephen Healy before the New York Stock
Exchange collapsed. He was the son of an RIC Sergeant and came
from a big family. When my mother wanted to do her village thing
where the Healys were concerned (which was most of the time), she
had plenty of scope, for there were thirteen of them in it. She first saw
the four Healy men walking behind their mother's hearse: she thought
them tall and handsome. Three of the brothers were indeed tall
enough and handsome enough to follow their father into the ranks of
the RIC. My father, Stephen, was the loner who never joined. Two
of them, Sonny and Joe, who later settled in Claremorris, came out
with Collins. Dick was stationed in Enniskillen when they drew the
border around the Six Counties. He had the option of waiting on in
the new force, the RUC, and did so. Years later, when Roy Bradford
chided me that you people in the South don't really understand us
Northerners, I was to tell him to genuflect carefully when he passed
Mount Pottinger RUC barracks where, to this day, they'll tell you
Head Healy was a good and fair police officer. (In the early Nineteen
Seventies when the Provo campaign was at its height, I made them a
present of that piece of family background. They would use it again
and again, and, when it became obvious that I would never apologise
– on the contrary – or deny the blood of my own, they settled for sending my newsprint writings to my mother, having first relieved themselves on the pages.)

  She could be as tough as I was. It was not until she was in her grave
that I learned she had been subjected to that piece of savagery by "the
lads". She forbade the family to tell me or mention it. Ever.

20

On the other hand, there was the famous time that our local Dáil Deputy, Joe Lenihan, got up in the Chamber and, having watched Garret FitzGerald, then in Opposition, pop up and down with a stream of questions to all and every Fianna Fáil Government Minister in front of him, Lenihan felt himself moved to observe that "You're up and down there like a whore's knickers", and I recorded it in the *Irish Times*.

My wife Evelyn and I were down home six months afterwards and my mother tore into me. "You should be ashamed of yourself: you never learned that language in this house – turn out your pockets there: I'll bet you haven't a Rosary beads in them."

I was forty years old and well married: Evelyn might have been embarrassed, as I most certainly was, but my mother wouldn't let it go. Nor was it any use protesting that I was merely quoting what the man said.

"Suff go deo[9] on him – you shouldn't have heard him." She had little time for the old Healy house in Bellaghy and, even less, it seemed, for the Healys. When she went in there, she'd say afterwards, the nettles were growing up their backsides and they were too lazy to wash themselves. All the same, when she had a hard birth with me, the first of the family, and complications developed ("I damn near died with you"), it was her sister-in-law, Dotie, who took me and nursed me.

My mother could be very confusing betimes. One day she'd never forget Dotie and the way she came to her help. Another day it'd be "That strap, Dotie . . . skiting off to dances until all hours of the mornin'", and so on.

Well, Dotie did get her man in Matt McDermott and she settled in Ballymote where she produced a fine family: they are a credit to her today.

My mother was death down on dancing and "the pictures" and it would be many many years later that I would understand why: in 1919-20 she had been a nurse during the devastating flu which swept the world and New York in particular. At that time the metropolitan

9. Bad cess to him.

health authorities had blamed film theatres, dance clubs and such centres of amusement as the hothouses of infection: it was there the flu bug struck down the thousands, and made all who attended such places not only victims but carriers of the virus as well. She had never forgotten that dreadful time and now in Ireland it was another virus which haunted us in the 'Thirties and 'Forties. Tuberculosis may not have been as sudden and as ravaging as The Plague of the Spanish Lady which struck and killed swiftly, but "the buck", as it was called, or "galloping consumption", was just as dreaded. For whatever reason, my mother wanted the minimum of public contact and only the parish church was deemed safe.

She had a similar passion for hygiene. There are old people in the town and countryside yet who remember her for that word: it was as if she invented it. It came hard on her to live without running water in Bellaghy and when she built the new house in Charlestown, on the edge of the town, she still had to go without the luxury of running water until, when she was retired, the water supply was extended and she availed herself of it hungrily.

She made do, the way they all did. You washed up as far as possible and down as far as possible and that was it. She had ewers all over the house: in two or three of them, she'd soften the water with orange skins steeped in river water. She had to have rain or river water: tap water was only for making tea. It was "too hard". And she loved toilet water: she sprinkled the bedspread each night before retiring.

One thing and one thing alone she ever gave the Healys and it remained a constant through thick and thin: "The Healys have brains – I'll say that much for them: they always had brains." My mother appreciated brains just as she was consumed with one constant, driving passion: her family would get an education. "You can go any place in the world once you have an education."

I was too young to know then, much less appreciate, that my mother had gone to America with nothing but a national school education from Cloonfane. She had seen the night-school system in Brooklyn, and driven Aunt Mary to see that her son John Flaherty was put through High School in Brooklyn. Her own early struggles in

Brooklyn imprinted the value of education on her: she had to make up a tremendous deficiency when she went to America, and was determined her children would not have to make the same struggle.

I never had much trouble in the early years at National School. I was born, it seemed, with a gift for spelling and reading. I was never conscious of a time when I couldn't read. Just as I never remember a time when I couldn't hum a Strauss waltz. It may be genetics: my father was a great old-time-waltz dancer and I remember how, later, he was always careful to pack his dancing pumps when he'd be taking us to Bundoran for the annual holiday. My mother wouldn't leave the district. Who'd look after the hens? She went thirty-five years without ever taking a holiday. There was always someone "due" – and if it wasn't that, the last resort was "the hens".

Bath night came two or three nights a week. The galvanised bath was put in the middle of the kitchen opposite the fire and filled with hot water: you stripped off and got in, and no modesty nonsense or giggles. She was death down too on lice or nits. Once we started school there was a nightly ritual in our house. You got down on your knees, put your head on her apron as she sat by the fire, and she took that ivory-comb and went through your hair with the thoroughness of a ferret. Every so often she'd stop.

"Hu-hu – who were you sitting beside today?" And you'd hear then the back of her nail crushing whatever it was she found with a vindictive pleasure. If you gave a name, you got a reply: "The bad breed – one of the seldom-feds – see you don't sit beside him tomorrow."

Two things you didn't miss in our house – the nightly hunt for nits and the Rosary, and in time she worked up as many trimmings as Grandma did in her day before her – and if you dared shuffle a chair you'd get a belt of that powerful citeog[10] of hers even in the middle of a Hail Mary. She never had any trouble mixing the prayer and discipline in one stroke.

You couldn't pick your companions in school, of course, for you sat as the places came to you. My mother didn't understand that. There were a few other things she didn't understand about the Irish

10. Left hand.

23

school system. Up to the senior room, life at school was a delight for me. I was, if anything, a bit precocious. If we had a spelling bee (a term I didn't know then) I was never worried: I knew whatever prize was going (generally a fistful of caramels or a sixpenny bit) was mine. Writing compositions was no trouble either.

My first trouble happened when I was "sent" to learn the piano. I loved and still love all kinds of music. There were two things wrong with piano lessons. The first was that it ate into your footballing time. The second, and more devastating as far as I was concerned, was that it was a mechanical affair. More correctly, it was a matter of giving mechanical values to each finger.

Reading music was simple enough. Hitting the notes was no problem. My trouble was that I had a habit of hitting the right notes with the wrong fingers. When that happened, my rather pudgy fingers got a belt of a cane or a ruler. I resented that deeply. I mitched on classes and, when the first pianoforte examination came up, all of them got first-class honours: I was the only one in the class to get second.

Those teaching methods maimed me for a long time, with the result that I detest mechanical rules. It was reinforced in the senior room when our teacher, with a somewhat similar approach, had his little "pantomime" each morning. It was Mental Arithmetic time. The teacher thwacking the cane against his trousers leg would say: "All right, gentlemen: we'll have a little pantomime and I'll play the drumsticks. Quickly, Healy – two and a half dozen oranges at three and ninepence a dozen." It was impossible. Unless you answered at rapid fire you got a slash of the cane. Very quickly your mind seized up: you didn't even hear the question as you figured out best how to dodge the inevitable belt. We were being asked to be human electronic calculators: it was never on, so you accepted, for that period, that it would be hell. It was.

It was pretty much the same with grammar, both English and Irish: it was taught in the same way. A word was fired at you: "Quickly, Healy – active or passive?" At least here you have a fifty-fifty chance – unless of course you were given two wrong choices and weren't quick enough to spot it was neither an adjective nor an adverb but a noun. I hated this mechanising of the language, Irish or English: this pulling it apart, word by word, for to me it stripped language of its beauty.

My real problem was that the anti-mechanical thing was developing in me. Up to now I had used words and constructed my sentences without any of this scaffolding of grammar. Write down an incorrect sentence or a misspelled word and before it was finished I had it corrected.

You knew instantly what was right and what was wrong. You could correct it and make it right. That, to me, was sufficient. But it wasn't sufficient for the educational system of the time, which demanded an ability to analyse and parse and decline. It often occurred to me, even then, that if we had to analyse and parse Christian Doctrine in the same niggling way, it might have killed a sense of religion and reverence in us.

My mother knew little enough of this system. As I moved towards sixth and seventh class I was constantly reminded that if I was to go on to secondary school I'd have to get a scholarship. Now at night I not only had to do my own lessons: I had to act as tutor to my younger brothers and sisters as well.

The "schol" – or scholarship – was about the most pernicious system ever devised by educationalists of those days. Places were few and the entry limited. My mother thought it was enough merely to be a pupil to be automatically entitled to compete. This was so in theory.

She knew nothing about the politics of the system. She didn't know or understand that the teacher, in practice, nominated those he thought fit to sit. Money was scarce and even schoolteachers who had large families had little enough in those days. One way or another it was generally the teachers' kids, or the kids of fellow teachers, who were on the inside track. The first year I was eligible, the teachers' sons from Charlestown were nominated. A cousin of mine from Ballymote, Meehaul Scanlon, the only child of John and Mollie Scanlon, took the top place and closed them out. The second and last year

I was eligible, it was a repeat and, again, another Healy cousin, Aunt Dotie's son from Ballymote, closed the next lot out again.

The Healys had brains all right but in the Nineteen Forties money was scarce in our house. There were five of us in it and the "stocking" my mother had brought home in the late 'Twenties was now exhausted. She had built two houses out of it: one in Castleduff and one in Charlestown. She had her salary as district midwife: my father was working as an agent for the Refuge Assurance Company but, more and more, his salary was eroded at each week end when he totted up all the sixpences and shillings he paid in for clients to save their policies from lapsing.

Few remember now the value these rural people set on the sixpence-a-week Insurance policy. They were basically funeral policies: they insured that the holders would have – no matter how hard times were – a coffin, a hearse and a shroud in which to be buried decently. The shilling that Ernest Blythe above in Dublin had taken off the old age pensioners created many a crisis for insurance men like my father in the decade before.

Later, when the amalgamation in the insurance industry came with the outbreak of war, the Irish Insurance offices would not give the Stephen Healys of rural Ireland the latitude of the old Refuge company. You lapsed the policies immediately if you didn't get your six-pence or shilling on the day and on the nail. My father was soft. He had grown up with these people and he knew how hard the times were. They knew little about insurance and its ramifications: theirs was the simple faith, akin to going to Mass – sixpence a week guaranteed you a decent funeral. Stephen Healy found it easier to dip into his own pocket for the defaulting sixpence or shilling to keep the policies alive until better days came. The years of cycling his district in all weathers were to take their toll. Now at the end of the 'Forties he was getting bad health. The good days were slowly coming back as MacAlpine's Fusiliers – as we called the emigrants – were sending home. They never quite came for Stephen Healy in a financial sense and when he died in 1952 at the age of 49, there would come, for a year or more, many of the sixpences and shillings that he had paid in for people who were now knowing better times even if his widow hadn't a share of them yet.

In 1944, things were already getting tight for my mother. Somehow, someway, we had to get an education because with an education you could travel the world. My two chances to sit for a scholarship had gone. There was little or no employment in the town itself. All there was – and it wasn't for townies like myself – was Cortoon Bog where, in the summer, Mayo County Council gave you four shillings and six-pence a day for saving turf. Well, if you couldn't get to St. Nathy's one way you could go the other way. If you had the fees (at that time, £45 a year), you'd be taken.

Two summers on Cortoon Bog would pay your way and, if you had any doubts about your townie status or worried about being called a "bogman", my mother straightened that out. "Better men than ye went on the bog in their day. There's nothing wrong with it: it's good money. And when you have an education you can travel the world. Off out with you on Monday morning and I'll put it a-by for ye and you'll get a schooling yet."

Cortoon, as I would soon learn, was an education in itself.

CHAPTER FIVE

That first Monday morning I set off to Cortoon, exhilarated. I passed Lowpark National School and the sense of freedom was absolute. I could almost hear the sharp, articulated voice of the teacher pounding his favourite clichés into the class to be used in every composition, no matter what the subject. "It was a fine autumn morning with a slight touch of frost mingled with the promise of a glorious day." Mine would be the only essay copy never to repeat his "descriptive passages", for I preferred my own attempts.

It didn't make me very popular with him and he could belt me when I denied his charge of cogging a simple sentence like: "Cats love to bask in the sun." At fourteen apparently you weren't supposed to know the word "bask". He would have been happier had I said "Cats love to lie in the sun." I couldn't explain to him then that I had my own instinct for words and that "bask" was a much better word than plain "lie": it suggested heat and languorous comfort.

Well, that was behind me now with all his autumn mornings and the touch of frost mingled with the promise of a glorious day. This was my glorious day and it needed none of John's frost to make it a promising one.

I had four miles to walk to Cortoon. I had my billy-can, my naggin of milk and my bacon and egg sandwiches. The bacon and egg was important, for in our house it was only my parents enjoyed bacon and eggs. They had their own table and they dined first and together. We breakfasted on a bowl of porridge, tea and bread at a second table. When we brought a lunch to school it was bread and jam. So that to get two sandwiches of bacon and eggs, you were somehow more

28

adult. I had my bacon and egg sandwiches in my old school bag. They had been prepared with a lot of care by my father. Bog work was hungry work, he'd say, packing the streaky rashers in between the slices. The eggs were soft and by lunchtime the yolks would have seeped into the rasher and bread. It didn't matter: it would be sweet eating.

The ganger was a townie like myself. We used to say he was four-foot-nothing "an' a right crabeen". His voice rasped. He would stand on the turf-bank and no camp commander in Colditz or Buchenwald was more vigilant. When you were turning turf or footing it and you went to straighten your back to ease the pain, he was on to you. You'd hear him a mile away shouting: "Haaaiiillleeey, bend that back." I learned very rapidly how to draw him so that when the command rang out, I'd straighten up to attention in apparent surprise, to protest: "But I have it down, sir." Even that brief three or four seconds eased the ache which, in the first two weeks, was absolutely deadly.

"Don't give me any of your backanswers – or you'll go up that road."

"That's right, Jim," someone would say, between his legs, and always it was "a rager sham", one of the country lads, who resented the townies working alongside them. They "Jimmed" him, something we wouldn't and couldn't do and the ganger didn't care too much for being "Jimmed" by anyone.

But Jim was all right once you got to know him and he was a lot less of a worry than the rager shams like John Mickey Morley, Anthony Corley or the Macs.

Before I started I had done what the whiz-kids now call basic market research. One or two of the lads had done a season in Broguey Bog in Sligo and we pumped them for information.

"There's no trouble to it, Healy: don't worry – just learn how to keep the Council Step."

The "Council Step" is a famous rural institution and years after-wards in Dublin, Donogh O'Malley, in the Board of Works, used always quote Paddy Smith's version of it as he was flying over Cork. Beneath him he saw black dots and a friend asked him what they were.

"Watch them for half an hour", says Paddy, "and if they move they're crows and if they don't they're Council workers."

Well, Nicko Walsh defined the Council Step for me: "Don't kill the job. Take it easy. Don't be in a hurry, and never break the line going up a bank of turf."

So off we went to Cortoon Bog with our heap of sandwiches and the billy-can for the brew-up of tea, bright and early on a Monday morning. We walked past Johnny Cassidy's school and with a great sense of relief that that was finished with – him and his glorious autumn mornings . . .

Jim McKeown was there before us looking at his watch, waiting for the hour hand to read the stroke of nine in the morning. "All right, men, it's time to start – ye'll take that first bank and start at the far end and work up."

As we moved to take up position and Jim went to shelter the bike from the sun by sliding the wheels into a cool drain, I got my first earful of squishy turf.

"Who did that?"

"Did what?" said John Mickey, his eye gleaming at the direct hit.

"Who . . ."

I never finished the sentence, for now the second ear was full and a third lump whizzed by the top of my head.

"Cut that out", I shouted.

"Stop that talking, Haaaiiillleeey."

Jim had stowed his bike for the day and was now ready to supervise us. I wanted to protest but an instinct told me I'd be wasting my time.

We started in a line at the top end of the bank. There were nine of us, all teenagers, two of them girls. But the townies were outnumbered seven to two.

Turning turf is no great problem: you simply move the sod to a new position, putting the exposed side down and turning up the sopping side to dry in the sun. We used cut and save our own turf and it was no bother to me. I kept remembering Nicko Walsh's advice: "Don't kill the job, keep the line: take it easy." I was about to look up and check I was keeping the line when I caught a lump of turf right in the eye.

"Morley, you . . ."

"Haaaiiillleeey – keep down that back."

John Mickey chuckled and mimicked Jim McKeown's order just loud enough for me to hear it but so that it didn't carry to Jim.

Within half an hour, having collected a few more clouts of wet turf, I began to notice that the rager shams, John Mickey and Company, were now a yard or more in front of us. This made it marginally easier for John Mickey, who was a crack shot with the citeog, to pick me off with a fast shot between his legs. He could shoot from any angle and without lifting his back and he was so fast the movement was barely perceptible. As he turned the sod he was gouging a lump of it and even as the sod was falling into its new position, he had squeezed the turf hard and fired it. There was a marvellous fluidity to the whole thing which you had to admire even though you were on the receiving end.

The shots rarely hurt you because the turf was soft but you were getting the needle and that hurt a bit more. What I didn't understand just then was why John Mickey and Company were a yard ahead of us townies: surely they had heard about the Council Step and taking the job . . .

"Haaaiiillleeey, ye're falling behind: get a move on."

I checked the line again. John Mickey and the lads were going like beavers now.

"Come on, Haaaiiillleeey, didn't ye hear the man. Bend yer back."

It was John Mickey.

"Ah, them townies fed on loaf bread and herrin's can't work, man dear", said one of the Macs. Everything was "man dear" with him.

"Dip in the dip and lave the herrin' for your father."

"Sure a good feed'd stiffen the likes of him."

"Haaaiiillleeey, stop that talking."

The crabeen MacKeown was at it again.

John Mickey and his cronies were going like demons now and we were two yards behind. They were also, I noted, shortening their turn-ings by a sod a man, leaving us with a wider swarth of turf to turn.

The sun was hot and sky-high larks patterned the billowing shimmer of heat now rising from the bog with lark-song. I got a move on and before eleven I had closed the gap. John Mickey disappeared mysteriously for fifteen minutes and as he came back Anthony Jack looked up at Jim McKeown and he, too, disappeared. Then it was Margaret's turn and she was ten minutes. No one said anything, coming or going.

Well, it was none of my business so long as I kept my back down and kept the line. But John Mickey and his friends were not keeping the line: they were going like men on piece work and by the end of the morning we had finished that bank. The lunch break at one was a relief and the appetite was sharp but, sharp and all as it was, the first mad desire was to lie down straight to ease the pain in the back.

John Mickey had a rake of sandwiches and a bottle of milk and had got through them before the billy-can was boiled and now he was right for "a bit of fun". The first bit of fun was a direct hit on the boiling billy-can.

"Aw, Christ, who did that? – there's fun and fun in it but, jasus, that's no fun", John Mickey said, with mock pity.

Butter, you'd say, wouldn't melt in John Mickey's mouth and his eyes were as innocent as a baby's. I went for him. He was bigger and heavier than me and had a good year on me but I had enough of the needle and this had to come sooner or later anyway. I can still see the utter astonishment in his big blue eyes as I sprang on top of him; he had been sitting down and I jumped on him like a tiger, fists flailing. I hit him with everything, fists, head and knees. He buckled in pain and surprise: his nose was pumping blood and we were threshing around wickedly when Jim McKeown, hearing the huzzahs as the lads formed a ring around us urging John Mickey to get up and do me, came on the scene.

He took a quick look at the damage to John Mickey who was now covered in blubbering blood and decided I was the aggressor.

"Haaaiiillleeey, get up that road – go on; you're fired."

This time I wasn't taking it.

"He started it. Look at me can of tea – Morley here clouted it, like he's been clouting me all the morning."

Jim looked at the fire and the kiltered billy-can on which the white ashes were already settling.

"Did you do that Morley?"

"It fell over itself . . ."

"You're a bloody liar, Morley – I saw you clodding it."

"All right; that'll do." Then to me: "Have ye any more tea?"

"No – all I had was in it, drawing."

"Have you anything to drink?"

"A drop of milk is all."

"Here, bring your mug down here and have some of mine."

Jim might be a crabeen but he was all right in his own way.

That afternoon was a back-breaking one. The rager shams tried to bury us in the turf-bank, working like madmen. The next day it was the same: they were going wild working and it was pure slavery. So much so I told Nicko Walsh that evening up at the ball alley. He couldn't understand it: it wasn't that way in Broguey.

"I'm telling you, Walsh, it's hard work: we're going solid from nine to one and from two to six and not as much as one break: the back down all the time."

"Are ye coddin' me?"

"I'm tellin' ye – not as much as a break for a fag: it's bloody murder."

"And why don't you take a walk across the bog?"

"How d'ye mean, a walk across the bog?"

"Well, jays, you have to have a piss now and again, haven't you?"

The penny dropped. So that's where John Mickey and the boys were going so mysteriously. And here was I conscientiously saving it up for lunch-time or knocking-off time!

Walsh must have seen comprehension dawning in my face: "Jays, I used to go five or six times a day."

By the end of the week, in addition to being known as "Glauber Salts", I had found a way, quite accidentally, to slow the pace down to "the Council Step".

It was the morning after the Thursday night pictures in the Eureka Cinema. We all started on the line together and the ganger was away

33

at the other end of the bank. One of my fellow townies had missed the picture and was asking me what it was like. I gave it to him, reel by reel, foot by foot, corpse by corpse, and it took me about forty minutes or so.

"Will ye move them turfs?", Jim bawled.

I looked, half expecting to be a yard or two behind John Mickey and the rager shams. They were in a dead straight line with us. Then I realised there had been no clodding either.

Had they been listening to my account of how Buck Jones had captured the rustlers? I still had a reel in hand and I watched John Mickey. He was all ears. So was Anthony Corley and the rest.

That feature film had an extra Healy reel tacked on to it and they still kept the line.

From there on in it was very simple because I had been going to the pictures for years and I could remember every foot of Hopalong Cassidy, Tom Mix, Buck Jones, Gene Autrey and Charles Starret.

Any skill I have as a narrator was born as much on Cortoon Bog and developed a lot more maybe than it was to be developed in St. Nathy's College or anywhere else for that matter. The first lesson in the art of communication was as tough as any I've had subsequently, for you had to be good enough to hold an audience which was basically hostile and had only one aim in life: to see you and your fellow townies buried in the boghole so that you didn't threaten their bread.

After all, if they were ready to "clim the job" (or spoil it) by violating the law of "the Council Step" in order to break a townie's back and spirit, to hunt them back into the town, you had to be fairly good to break through that, and to win a grudging acceptance which slowed down that line. All through the turning and, later, through the footing and refooting and clamping of the turf I dictated the pace as I retold the stories of the films and went on from there to books I had read.

Actually I got to like John Mickey Morley very well, for he was a big soft buttermilk lad with a great streak of devilment in him and a most marvellous pair of blue eyes which were spring wells of smiles.

But the old town-country animosity sprang to life again in the late summer when it came to "putting out" time.

This was real money for if you had an ass and a pair of pardógs[11] (or creels) you got the princely sum of six and sixpence for walking behind an ass, as compared with four and sixpence a day for the backbreaking job spreading, turning or footing turf.

An ass costs £40 in rural Ireland today but I picked up Silver for thirty bob at Howley's Corner of a fair day. It never occurred to me to look to see if the ass was a full jack, a cut jack or a mare and it turned out that Silver (named after Buck Jones's famous steed) was a mare. Well, I had her home by this time and it was all a one, I thought. You could ride to work now in the morning on Silver, a bouncy new pair of sally rod creels bobbing up and down as Silver did her brisk trot to Cortoon. Nicko Walsh had advised me about the form.

See the ass kept the Council Step and don't let them lift the creels off the straddle, to throw the sods upon the turf stack. Empty the sods one by one by hand: throwing the creels, full, on the turf stack "climmed" (or broke) them. And finally: keep the line. Don't spoil the job.

John Mickey and the rager shams didn't believe a townie would ever think of buying an ass and creels: where would you keep an ass within in the town?

That was no problem: there was the field behind our own house where we played football; there was the field at the Alley, a sort of commonage, and finally the Doctor's Field with lush grass. So that when I sailed down the road with Silver and the creels John Mickey very honestly told me I was "rimming it now".

It didn't matter a damn to me: I was making me bobs and was now well able to hold my own if it came to a fist fight with John Mickey or any of the rest of them. I might be as thin as a whippet but I was fairly wiry and though I hated to fight, if someone got up on my back, I'd go for him. John Mickey had no cause for complaint: he was there with his ass and creels, wasn't he?

The usual country trick was tried: the sods would be smashed into the bottom of the creels by the loaders and some of the men on the

11. Creel which opens underneath.

turf stacks on the public Dublin-Ballina road wanted to lift the creels off and wallop them down, sods and all, on the reek. That would soon wear them out and, they hoped, put me out of business. But I was ready for that and wouldn't have it. Those creels will be emptied like John Mickey's, sod by slow sod. That way the job lasts longer for us all. But I was vulnerable and my vulnerability was in Silver and her sex. John Mickey – naturally! – was the first to get the message and no better man.

I had noticed myself that Silver seemed suddenly to develop a habit, when I jumped on her back, of putting her head down, her lugs back, and opening her mouth noiselessly, as if she was silently protesting something or other. She was slow to move: indeed she wouldn't move for me until I got off her back, gave her a dunt in the tail, and smartened her up a bit. John Mickey's ass, a thundering great big black jack-ass, was even livelier than usual and I noticed that as I was going back empty, John's ass, his ears cocked forward like Arkle, was violating not only the code of the Council Step as he came out, loaded down: he was positively prancing towards Silver and seemed as reluctant to pass her as Silver was to pass him. And Silver put her head down and opened her mouth as if she was braying silently.

"Drive out them asses", Jim McKeown bawled at both of us. Reluctantly the asses responded to our reins.

John Mickey, however, was smiling richly to himself. It was a devilishly lecherous smile, as if he knew something I didn't know. Now part of the Council Step thing was that you put your ass a-bogging. This meant sinking her in a soft spodach[12] turf bank to her hocks. That killed fifteen minutes while you emptied the creels, pulled the ass up by the head and tail, straddled her again, put on the creels and reloaded. If you give an ass his head, he'll never go a-bogging: he can smell the soft conditions and avoid them. So you had to work at it. One trip in four was a "bogging" trip and again I noticed this silent braying of Silver and her contentment to lie there as we pulled her up and loaded.

At the lunch break the devastating truth broke on me when I heard

12. Spongy white turf.

36

John Mickey telling Anthony Corley "Hailey's ass is in hate – we'll have a bit of fun if our one gets to her." John and Anthony were having their bite around the other corner of the turf-stack.

I looked around in a panic. Silver was grazing away, the straddle on her back and John Mickey's jack was down the bog. Thank God for that! I bolted my lunch and got up to get Silver. Just then John Mickey and Anthony darted from the other side of the turf-stack, quite obviously going to collect Silver and bring her down the bog. I got there first, grabbed the bridle, put the bit into her mouth and took possession of her.

"Go on – leave my ass alone", I said, turning on them.

"Sure we're doin' nothin' with your ass", said John Mickey full of innocence.

"Go on", said Mick Henry, a lad from the edge of the town but who lined up with me: "keep that jack to yourself, Morley." Mick knew the game: that John Mickey wouldn't rest until his jack-ass got to my mare.

For three tortured days I watched Silver like a hawk, helped by Mick Henry and some of the other lads from the town. We split the dangerous lunch-shift when, with the creels off, Silver was most vulnerable.

At the end of the third day we were on the last load, for it was chucking time. This was not only the fastest load of the day when the donkeys and drivers seemed miraculously to find great energy: it was the only time you let the men at the turf-reek on the side of the road take the creels off and throw them up on the reek to empty them, so that you could get away home in double quick time. I didn't see John Mickey and his jack-ass behind me. The creels came off and I was watching to see they weren't banged too hard when John Mickey's jack, seeing his chance, took it.

No virgin ever defended her honour as viciously as I tried to save Silver: I hit out blindly with my ashplant at the slavering black jack-ass. He still had the creels on his back and John Mickey was fighting desperately to get them off him to make it easier for him. Blows across the head did nothing to him and now, with the creels off and John

37

Mickey trying to stop me from hitting him, I had to take on John as well. The boys, of course, enjoyed it all, for by now John Mickey and Anthony Corley had overpowered me and I had to stand there watching.

I can still remember the revulsion and frustration. Silver, at least, could escape if she'd only run for it. But to my horror she was making no attempt at all: she had her head down, her lugs back and her mouth was open in that silent bray I had noticed all week when I jumped on her back.

Behind us, a horn sounded. It had to be the Dublin-Ballina bus! So it was: it was held up, for the asses blocked the road. And naturally the front seats had to be occupied by two Convent of Mercy nuns: dutifully, they turned their modest gazes away from this roaring rural orgy. The driver, on the other hand, accepted the inevitability of it all. Propping his elbows on the steering wheel he watched it all with a benign and amused understanding which infuriated me – couldn't he at least do something to save Silver? That driver knew his job. For just as John Mickey's black jack delivered the final thrust, he gentled the gear lever into first and had the bus moving forward slowly as John Mickey's jack, limp and spent, fell back exhausted.

John Mickey half released me: he was satisfied now and so were his neighbours. A town mare had been raped well and truly by the best black-jack in all of Cortoon! There was nothing much I could do now but accept it.

It would be twenty-five or more years later I would pass this spot again with my wife. I was driving my first Rolls Royce into Charlestown for the first time. I stopped and told my wife: "This is where it happened. It took as much courage for me to drive an ass and creels out to this bog twenty-five years ago as it's now going to take me to drive this bloody car into Charlestown: do you understand that?"

She understood.

On balance now Silver and the creels were probably the better investment, for, pregnant though she was, she was the passport to St. Nathy's for me the next summer. For my mother had been as good as her word: she had "put a-by" the savings of my younger brother, Kevin, and myself and in the autumn of 1945 we both went to St. Nathy's together to get the education which would let us travel the world and make a reality of her driving ambition for us.

Pat O'Neill sent home the new suits and shirts and 50 dollars to help with books and Mary Flaherty sent a cheque, too, and wished us well.

We were on our way – and no one ever went to Nathy's with as fixed a purpose as I did. I was going to be a journalist, come hell or high water . . .

CHAPTER SIX

My mother, as I said, was death down on dancing and "the pictures". Growing up, I thought it was something to do with the Healys. All the Healys were great dancers.

"That's all they were ever good for – that an' gallivanting", my mother would say. It would be many many years later that I would come to understand the dread she had of enclosed places of entertainment like a dance hall or a cinema. It was a throw-back from her days in the Great Flu epidemic which she and her sisters had fought in New York in the closing days of the First World War, when a whole city went round with flu masks and when, too, all places of entertainment were closed down in a desperate fight to ward off the unseen virus which was to claim, all over the world, the lives of at least 21,000,000 people of all nations, creeds and colours.

She was in the thick of it in New York and saw strong men drop dead in the streets of Brooklyn when the epidemic was at its height. Now in the 'Forties in Ireland it was another fear. The flu bug had died, but tuberculosis – "the buck", or galloping consumption – was as feared in rural Ireland then as the Spanish Lady epidemic was feared twenty years before. Public places like dance halls and cinemas were unhygienic and spread "the buck": as with the flu virus, you didn't know who was a carrier.

It may, of course, have been a mother's awareness that her first son was coming to adolescence and therefore had to be watched. And since we had been educated in segregated classes, our contact with girls was very limited. In church, the women took one side, the men the other and the children were seated in the centre pews. We had a brief flirtation with co-education in our town at secondary level but it was considered a mortal sin of some kind and ended before I was ready to go to that school. O'Malley's mini-buses and falling numbers make the educational mortal sin of the Nineteen Forties an educational necessity and virtue in the Nineteen Seventies and now boys and girls mix and mingle with a greater ease. It may be that they are still as tongue-tied as we were in the face of beauty in those days – and tongue-tied we were.

It had nothing to do with class distinction because there is no class distinction as such in rural Ireland: there is a hierarchical structure which any village or town must have – a pecking order. It is a different thing from class distinction.

It is true we elevated our women to an exalted plane: in Sunday sermons the message about chastity and purity was belted home. Man was an animal and his animality defiled himself and his woman: we must fight it. The Children of Mary, in their virginal blue cloaks, going demurely to the altar, served all the more to remind you of the Adam-cursed animality and unworthiness of the male.

And they were all lovely girls to look at as they walked down from the altar after Communion and later, with eyes modestly on the footpath, down Chapel Street, Main Street or up Barrack Street. Butter wouldn't melt in their mouths and even the very thought of trying it to see if it did, seemed repugnant. And so you kept your distance and sighed – a process which was helped greatly when pocket money was all too scarce and it took a lot of engineering to corner a "pass out" so as to get into the dance for nothing of a Sunday night where it might all happen for you if you were lucky.

Dancing in those days, was a very innocent affair as far as I was concerned. I happened to be a very good dancer by the time I was sixteen and enjoyed it so much that it was an end in itself.

The girls stood at one end and the boys at the other end and when the band started you made a race across the floor for a favourite partner. You danced the round and when the music stopped you both went back to your corrals to "study form" for the next dance. One girl was a good old-time waltz partner, another a dab hand at the slow

41

waltz, yet another very good at the quick-step or the quick fox-trot. The only trouble was that your friends knew, too, who was good and if you lost the race across the floor you had, sheepishly, to settle for another partner and take pot-luck. Inevitably there were always girls who never got a turn and who stood wallflowered all night. It was all good clean fun.

Some girls had a Legion-of-Mary way of holding a partner, keeping you at a distance, and some girls had a very comfortable way of appearing to mould themselves to you so that the pair of you danced as one person. Now and again, in a slow dance and with the lights down to a romantic glow, a Legion-of-Mary partner was known to change her style. She might breathe a bit more heavily now that she was closer and the bantering chit-chat seemed to dry up as if she were concentrating. But when the lights went on you were back to the corral again, spotting form for the next round. You might be walking home contented after a good night's dancing and three girls or four, seeing you on your own in the dimly lit street, might ask with a laugh why you were going home on your own – didn't you meet anyone you liked better than yourself? And you said something and went your contented way.

You heard of girls who were "a good hoult" or "a good squeeze". Others were "bicycles" who'd "eat a man" but you were not interested and you didn't believe it.

Mercifully it was not always like that and, sooner or later, there came the girls who enjoyed something more than a good dancing partner and who knew how to take the initiative when the fellow she wanted was too green to read the signs she was giving him on the floor. She was being pestered by so-and-so and he wanted to leave her home and she was afraid of him; would you ever mind walking her to the house? She knew it was out of your way a bit but . . .

Not at all, you'd be delighted.

And you were . . .

Sweet sixteen and never been kissed.

Well, you were going to be kissed now and you were. Even then with an eager young lassie moulding her sweet young body around you

42

in the warm darkness, one half of you was standing back remembering her in her Child of Mary blue veil, demure eyes cast down, and the awful words of warning about the animality of man (now stirring full-bloodedly) ringing in your mind. You were caught in the old lovely delirium. You would pay for this but not yet . . . All you hoped was that she could not spot the rising animality which would brand you as a defiler.

But no matter how you shifted gears with your knees, the sinuous eager body, which had followed every inventive step on the dance floor, now worked itself closer.

The mouth was opened invitingly and you could think of nothing then but Silver in heat, her mare's lugs thrown back and her mouth open as John Mickey's jack raped her on the Cortoon Road.

I survived that and many another night as I learned that girls in these dancing towns of Mayo and Sligo could be as passionate as male animals and that while they might be demure and superbly modest of a Sunday morning, they could, God bless them, be healthy young ones on Sunday night.

Of course by the following Saturday night they were another thing entirely. You paid heavily in agonising as you moved up the queue, one place nearer to the dark confessional box. Your heart thumped in fear as the slide on the grill opened. You got rid of the ordinary pedestrian sins first. Then you got your cue:

"Anything else, my child?"

"I kept company, Father."

"With a girl?"

"Yes, Father."

"Well, did anything happen?"

"I kissed her, Father."

"Did she kiss you back?"

"She did, Father."

"Were you both passionate?"

"We were, Father."

"Did you touch her indecently?"

"No, Father."

43

"Did you have an erection?"

"Yes, Father."

Pause.

"Did you a -er spill the seed?"

"Some of it, Father."

"I see."

Pause again.

"Are you going to marry this girl?"

"I don't know, Father."

"Are you keeping steady company with her?"

"Sort of, Father."

"And you intend to go on seeing her?"

"I think so, Father."

Pause again; there is a heavy sigh from the darkness.

"Well, now, look. You have to do something to control your urges: they are natural urges between a boy and a girl but they are to be kept for marriage. Outside marriage it is sinful and you are both making it an occasion of sin. You should try and stay out of dark places: be with other young people; that will lessen the temptation. Try not to be alone. And go regularly to the sacraments and pray that God will give you strength to resist these temptations."

Another pause.

"Now tell God you are sorry for your sins. Say the rosary three times for the next three days . . . Oh my God . . ."

And he gave you absolution once again, slid back the slide and sent you, once again, light-hearted and relieved on your way. The chapel was brighter now that your soul was shriven, and the candles on the offertory box positively gleamed with joy where before, in the dark, they seemed sullen and dull.

You could die tonight but your soul was spotless.

Tomorrow morning you would be at the rails and some of the demure girls would be at the rails and for all of this day there would be brightness and life and sunshine.

The Rosary and Benediction on Sunday evening would come and the girls would be there and you wondered if they were going dancing

44

this night or whether the Canon had told them it was an occasion of sin and it must stop now once and for all.

And once again you found yourself promising that if your girl of the moment came you'd be good for both of you and you'd see that "nothing happened". But even as the Host was being raised in a blessing, you knew at the back of your mind that when the dance was over you would have that supple young body pressing close to you and moulding itself about you and you would leave her, knowing that you would have to face the Canon again with the same old story, hear the same old patient words of advice, make the same old act of Contrition with the old gratitude and leave the confessional box with a firm act of resolution to try and do better the next time.

We never did and if we didn't, we did no damage either except maybe make our women wonder what kind of stiff sticks we were.

Looking back now, we must have irritated many of them, and frustrated some of them, by being Sixth Commandment prigs.

And that attitude must have been common enough for there used to be a deadly vicious saying in our rural society to describe such people: "you'd die at the hole like a poisoned rat."

It was a corrosive rural taunt and its regular usage – and the withering effect it always had – suggests to me now that the generality of us treated the girls of our day with the devotional respect we were told was due to them.

You learned things for yourself and you learned, in time, that there was such a thing as "nancy boys".

The nearest thing I ever got to sex instruction was a warning from my mother to be sure never to be alone with so-and-so – and she left it at that.

I was supposed to know and, of course, I did. In a small community, deviant behaviour of any kind becomes public property in a matter of hours and loses nothing in the telling.

There was supposed to be an incident but whether it ever happened remained a matter of doubt and certainly community pressures ensured that it was never repeated: the subject faded into the background for me. When it came up again, I was to be a lot less detached about it.

45

It was to be in the closing weeks of my brief stay in St. Nathy's. I had been in a row with one priest and had forced him to go to the President on the matter of corporal punishment. Challenging authority for a schoolboy is a dangerous policy, but I would not flinch. You may win, but you must know there will, some time, be a price to pay. There was evidence that I was a reasonably average student with a flair for a few subjects like English, Latin and Science. Now it was Inter Week and most of the students who were not taking exams had gone home. It was traditional that discipline was relaxed: the rule of solemn silence was not strictly honoured. After all it was June and the evenings were long and bright until almost midnight. In an open dormitory we moved around and shared parcels from home. Because my brother and I started together, we had a double bed at one end of the wide open dormitory. Kevin was down the dormitory talking to some friend of his; a friend of mine was sitting on the end of my bed, on top of the bedspread, discussing the careers we would both have in journalism.

The door opened quietly. The President walked in and looked around the dormitory. He said nothing. People out of bed walked back to their own beds and, still without a word, the President turned on his heel and left.

None of us worried about it. It was Inter Week after all. Indeed inside half an hour we were all talking again except for the few who were "swotting up".

It was lunch-time the following day when the bomb went up. My friend, Seán, who had been sitting on the end of our bed, told me he had met the President, who had asked him what his parents would think of his conduct?

Seán had replied: "Well, Canon: they know it was Inter Week." "And what will they think when they learn their son is a homosexual?"

Seán was very serious and not at all given to being melodramatic: he told me he had denied it but he felt sure the President did not accept it and intended to report the matter to his parents. It didn't take me too long to realise that if the President was accusing Seán of being a homosexual, then I had to be the consenting second party.

I wasn't going to wait for the President and his filthy sick mind. Just then the Dean of Discipline came through the gate to the back walk: immediately Seán and myself flanked him and I related the incident. I told him that unless the President apologised and withdrew the allegation, I would go to the Bishop, after that to the Cardinal and after that, if my family had to, to a civil court of law for damages.

The Dean pointed out very gently that I had not been so accused by the President and the matter did not arise. I thought it did; now was he prepared to take that message to the President or did I have to go myself?

He was a decent little man who had once caught me smoking (for which I could have been expelled on the spot) but he put me on my honour not to smoke again: I had enough regard for his understanding and decency that I didn't smoke.

But this one, plainly, was something else and he was disturbed and worried. In the end he found a solution of a kind. Why not take the matter up with the Spiritual Confessor: it was really his field, after all.

Seán wasn't sure: the Spiritual Confessor wasn't exactly the most popular man in the house. More correctly, his room was the one room in the House we all avoided: no one wanted to be seen entering, or leaving, "Snig's" room. The nickname was supposed to suggest that, as you passed, he reached out and "snigged" you in and lectured you on the facts of life.

To be fair, the man had the unpleasant Irish task of providing some sort of sex education to young fellows reaching puberty. There circulated among the more knowing Snig's test: when he put his hand gently on your knee, they said, you wanted to be sure your old man wouldn't swell and stiffen or Snig would know too much.

The myths, of course, were, as always, a travesty: he was a very cheerful fatherly figure of a man who was also – or so he conveyed to you – a man of the world who understood all these trifling problems associated with growing up and you weren't to worry.

I doubt, however, if he was quite prepared for my story that June day. I repeated what I had said to the Dean of Discipline: either the charge would be withdrawn and an apology made or I would see to it I went right through the process to a court of civil damages.

He was an urbane man and he sought to calm me down. It was smooth. We committed many sins in secret and got away with them and were never punished but sometimes God sent us crosses when we were accused of sins of which we were innocent and God expected . . . "Look, Father, I understand about crosses but one cross I will not carry is the charge of being a homosexual – now do you give my message to the President or do I do it myself? I am serious: my parents will take this all the way to the courts. I am prepared to go down to the Oratory with you, or anyone else, and swear in the presence of the Blessed Sacrament that it is a lie, and a filthy lie at that."

He asked me to leave it with him: he was sure there was a mistake. He would see the President. That evening the President sent for Seán. He withdrew the charge and apologised. The matter would end with that.

For Seán it did. But not for me.

In the warm June sunshine of Revision Week you sat out in the recreation grounds and swotted up. I was at the end of the walk the next day swotting up Irish grammar. I had, as usual, a novel in my inside jacket pocket but I was swotting up an Irish Grammar. The President cat-footed his way from his spy-hole in the Top Oratory. Once he appeared at the Gate, you got up and circulated as you were supposed to be doing. He stood and waited for you to pass him. Inevitably he called "Mister Healy" over and reached into my inside jacket pocket. "You were reading."

"Yes, Canon. My Irish Grammar."

By this time he had fished one of the two books out. It had to be the sixpenny Mellifont cowboy. "Your Irish Grammar – I thought as much."

But just as coolly I reached in and fished out my Irish Grammar. His eyes were cold – but no colder than mine as I looked straight at him and said slowly: "I was reading my Irish Grammar." He nodded his head sideways to dismiss me to carry on walking.

The next morning we were to start the all-important examination, on which my mother had set such store. I had completed The Thirty

Days Prayer, like everyone else, that I'd get this examination and that I would not have to listen to my mother crying about all "my hard-earned money gone for nothing". We were finishing breakfast when, unusually, the President walked into the Refectory, slapped his breviary for attention and announced that some boys – and they know who they are – may not be allowed to sit for all of these examinations. They know they have been under observation and that their misconduct entitled him to expel them now or at any time in the next few days. Their conduct was insolent; their lack of respect for authority was well known. He would deal with them at any time from now on and they could be removed from the examination hall at any time. With which words, he disappeared.

Half an hour later I was at my desk in the examination hall. It so happened that the desk was partially hidden by the folded partitions which had been moved back to make one large room. The President came over: "Mister Healy, would you please move your table into the centre here – it will remove the temptation to copy." It was said with a dry wintry smile – or as near as a wintry smile ever got to that poor man's twitching lips.

Very levelly I said: "As you say, Canon, though I am sure you will have noticed that my marks have been fairly consistent over the past three years." I was getting the needle and if he was going to throw me out anyway, at least I wouldn't go without a fight. He had not apologised to me over the dormitory incident and that was one card I still held and I knew it. It was a long and tension-filled week but none of us were pulled out and expelled. Now it was all over and the summer was ahead of us, days of freedom.

The President stook at the top of the Refectory to shake hands with each of us as we filed out. At my turn he merely looked at me coldly: I returned that look, pausing for a split second, and walked on.

I collected my bags, walked out the gate, left down my bags and looked back. I gave the place the soldier's farewell, learned in Renmore Barracks, Galway, the previous year as an FCA man. I never had any doubt that June day in 1948 that I would be anything other than a newspaper man. I would have to fight with my mother who would want me to return to "finish your education" so that I could travel anywhere in the world.

I would have to outflank her.

I sneaked my Sunday clothes out the window one Friday morning so as not to alert her, borrowed a neighbour's bicycle and, with the equivalent of ten new pence in my pocket, set off for Ballina and the offices of *The Western People* 25 long miles away. I would be turned away by the manager who would tell me the editor wasn't in and, anyway, they weren't hiring anyone. I would wait on Ham Bridge in Ballina for four hours watching the fresh salmon jump in the Moy, to throw the sea lice off them. At five that evening I got through the manager to see the editor Fred de Vere. He liked what I had written and offered me a start at £1 a week. I would have to stay in Ballina. Digs would be £2.25 pence.

The journey home was longer and I knew there would be a fight. Where had I been all day? Had I asked permission? How did you get that suit on you? I never answered. I was going to bed. My mother wasn't used to this manner, of not getting an answer. Was it possible I was drinking? "Come over here until I smell your breath", she said.

I knew it was pointless but I let her do it. Doubly annoyed now when there was no smell of drink on me, she unleashed her powerful left hand at what she took to be my studied insolence.

I was too tired after the round trip of 50 miles to care and far too tired to get into the fight I knew had to come. She had me up early the next morning and marched me into my father's bedroom to explain myself for my absence the previous day. "He'll deal with you", she said. My very gentle and easy-going father heard me out and long before I got to finish my story I knew I was away with it.

He remembered Cahir Healy, MP, offering to have me indentured with Robert Kirkwood of *The Irish News* in Belfast when the time came. Cahir had encouraged him to think I had the makings of a newsman. My mother came in, hands on hips, as I was finishing my case: to return to St. Nathy's for a further two years would be pointless when I would have to start as a cub reporter; the school fees which would be saved could subsidise my accommodation in Ballina and, at the end of the two years, I'd be that much more on the road and probably able to support myself.

"Well?" asked my mother, annoyed I wasn't at least on the floor and showing signs of having been through the wars. My father explained the situation.

"You're softer than he is – he's going back to finish his education. He'll be a doctor – we're not wasting all our hard-earned money on him that he isn't going to finish. I wouldn't mind – but there's not even a pension in it. What are you going to do in your old age and no pension? You'll go back to college and finish or I'll see you dead first. Mara faisc[13] on you and your newspapers. Get out now, till I talk to your father here."

I got a fair going over for two days after that but my father's view held and within the week he hired a taxi to bring me to Ballina; he checked the digs to see they were suitable.

A month later I brought in a story which made three front page splashes in Ireland and Fleet Street. I also got the results of the Intermediate and had got Maths, Irish, Latin, Science, History and Geography. I checked the English mark again: it was the highest of the lot.

Then I threw the lot in *The Western People* wastepaper basket. I was on my way and I knew it . . .

---

13. The death cloth.

CHAPTER SEVEN

These were the years when Castleduff slipped from my focus and the
warm world of summer farming on the hill began to fade. Even now
I am hard put to know when it started to change. Uncle Jim had
married Mary Anne before Grandma died and my mother was to say
that, with Mama's passing, the "nature" went out of the house.

Grandda was still there and the cats and the night crickets, and
Uncle Jim seemed to be as big and as jovial as ever. Grandda took to
the bed in the west room above the kitchen and in a long summer he
slipped away.

Mary Anne fussed over me as much as Grandma. She put down the
few Champions with the pig's pot of potatoes: she made bruisey in the
same way. And she worried more.

"Ora-wora-John-Joe- don't be climbing the hay, like a good
laddeen, for fear you might fall, agradh."

She had a bicycle and when she went to Charlestown she brought
back a bar of Fry's chocolate and a bag of Rainbow caramels. She
seemed to regard my mother with a pitiful respect: she was always
explaining and apologising to her and running to wipe the seat she sat
on, or the spot on the table, before she would put down a cup of tea.
Uncle Jim and my mother talked as equals: Mary Anne seemed in
some way to go in awe of them.

Things certainly changed when Cousin Edward and Bernie were
evacuated from England. They were Uncle Michael's sons and were
sent home to Ireland for safety, as war evacuees. They were a few
years older than me and spoke with a strong English accent I found
hard to understand. Edward had one song, "Any umbrellas to fix

today?'' and Bernie had one called ''A tisket-a-tasket-a-little-yellow-basket'', but they weren't, I thought, very bright about farming things. This place was ''very dead an' all'', not like ''over''. I didn't know where ''over'' was, beyond that it was somewhere in England. They never talked about their father or mother and they didn't have any of the games we had. Edward, we thought, was a bit ''loud'' and Bernie the quieter and more introspective of the two.

They settled in to farm life. Edward had a lot of misgivings about it but Bernie was a ''hard worker''. Bernie, too, they were to say, ''had more nature in him'' and that was a thing which it was important to have, it seemed.

The third season after Edward and Bernie arrived I was told by my mother that I couldn't stay in Carracastle for the summer and that was the first break. Uncle Jim had two mouths to feed and anyway Edward and Bernie needed ''my room''. Besides, I was now old enough to ''watch the baby'', for by now there were five of us in it, the last being Junie, making three boys and two girls. Apart from that, it was a long walk to Carracastle and with no Grandma to give you an enormous half-a-crown it wasn't worth it to walk out and back the one day; and there were undercurrents about Jim and Mary Anne which I never understood at the time.

Mary Anne had no children of her own. In the harsh language, she was a ''glugger'', the egg which never hatched out no matter how long the clocking-hen sat on it. There was a flurry of excitement which my mother shared when, for a time, it was thought Mary Anne was pregnant. Years afterwards when her dander was up over something in Carracastle, my mother would say: ''Is it that one? Sure she was never pregnant; she was as old as the crows when Jim married her. All that moaning and nonsense – it was 'the change' and I told her, too – she couldn't fool me.''

Nothing that poor Mary Anne ever did was right with my mother except one thing: she made butter as good as Grandma ever made it and below in Gavaghan's of Bellaghy, Mary Anne O'Donnell's butter never lasted five minutes after it was weighed on the scales and she was paid for it. In the years in which my mother was ''out'' with

53

Carracastle, we'd be sent down to tell Mamie Gavaghan to keep the next roll of Carracastle butter.

A neighbour might inquire how they were all in Carracastle and, depending on the degree of familiarity which my mother permitted, they'd be told. If they were from my mother's village and had grown up with her (but had married out of it) they could expect the confidences to be exchanged.

During these war years in the 'Forties you might be sieving brown flour through a muslin cloth for the luxury of a white soda cake when a village neighbour would come in with some small medical complaint and the confidences would start over a cup of tea. "Castleduff is a changed place since your mother went, Nora." (She had to be a village woman to call my mother "Nora": with non-village women it was "Nurse Haley" or "Missus Haley".) A sip of tea and then: "Do you go out at all now, Nora?"

"Now and again."

"Wasn't it an awful pity Jim never had a family: Mary Anne is beyond it now, I suppose?"

"She was beyond it the first day he married her. There's nothing wrong with our Jim – he left his mark well in . . ." And she named the village.

For a woman who was almost puritanical in many ways, as I discovered growing up, it always struck me as odd that she could admit to this. Later, when she had a feud going with Jim, she'd say he couldn't have luck, having got two girls into trouble during the Troubles.

Consistency was not my mother's strongest line and she could parade you for someone who called: "This is my son John, who is in journalism." Five minutes after they were gone, you'd be called down the banks for a wastrel who refused to go back to college to finish and be a doctor!

The village caller would wonder if Jim would leave the farm to Mikie's lads, Bernie and Edward, seeing as he had none of his own. "Them, is it? Sure they have no nature for the place and they wouldn't know what to do with it if they got it."

"You were a great woman, Nora, to put the slates on two houses for your time in America."

"And many a hard night I put in to do it but if I had my time again I'd be wiser."

"It would come hard on me, never mind you, if the long-tailed crowd from Barroe were ever to set foot in Castleduff, Nora."

Barroe was where Mary Anne came from and my mother didn't think a lot of the Barroes. In truth, she didn't think much of any village but her own; of any people but her own. I didn't know then what that village woman meant about my mother putting the slates on two houses for her time in America and indeed it was news to me that she had ever been to America. I didn't know, either, how my mother could be wiser if she had her time again. Evidently she had regrets about something or other and it seemed to be connected with Carra-castle and the farm.

My mother talked very little about America or her life there and she went no further back in time than that traumatic moment when, having married my father, she was to discover that "the nettles were up to the back door when I went into that house".

The Healys, she'd say, were always content to live with "the nettles up to the back door". The Healys had "no cutting" in them. "Cutting" was an important thing to my mother. It had to do with standards, with being independent, with keeping yourself to yourself. You didn't mix with every Tom, Dick and Harry. You didn't make a messenger boy of yourself for anyone. Which was really too bad because my father was the opposite of all these things.

Having an insurance book to collect, he'd look at "the run" every morning and, because he knew the small wants of every house, he would stuff his saddle bag with the ounces of plug tobacco, the quarter of tea, the bag of sugar and the packets of Woodbines for the "people out in the country". There were hard times, as I've said, when they couldn't pay their small weekly or monthly premiums and if the fairs were bad or the markets poor, my father would pay the shilling or two to keep the policy alive rather than "lapse" them. "Lapse" was a dreadful word to my father and when he had to let a policy lapse it

55

was a bad day, not because he lost a few pence commission but because he knew how hard it came on a decent country woman to have to let lapse a "funeral policy". You had to be desperate to let a funeral policy lapse and my father, who knew how much it meant, would try and keep the policy alive.

My mother had little time for that kind of thing and there were certain villages she had a set on and wasn't at all surprised to hear they couldn't pay their premiums. She'd let them pay their own premiums – and run their own messages, too.

"Small thanks you'll get", she'd say, "making a messenger boy of yourself for that crowd. I'd let them run their own messages: suff go deo on them but they never had anything there anyway."

But my father let it in one ear and out the other and his saddle bag would be full and his pocket lighter at the end of many a day as he cycled the hills and bog roads to collect the book.

My mother held that he was "too soft" and she wouldn't be like that: every time she was called on a "a case", she had her fee. She stood for "no nonsense" with patients in the district and they knew where they stood with her. If they wanted her, they'd pay for her, she wasn't cycling the hills at all hours of day and night without getting paid.

She was, of course, a professional nurse and had the reputation of having lucky hands: she rarely lost a child at a confinement and she was to deliver two generations of women in that district.

But she could not change my father who would, to the end of his days, continue to be "too soft", paying these small premiums, bringing out the bit of tobacco or some other small comfort, and often having nothing for it but the prayers of some of these people.

When, to balance his books, he had to dip into his salary, it produced more tensions at home.

With the outbreak of war, the Refuge Assurance Company was taken over by an Irish group and in the business things got a lot worse. For now instead of gentle Cahir Healy, the Enniskillen MP, coming once a quarter, it seemed to us that our house was now an eating house for a horde of ranking bods who never brought anything to us and took everything they could get.

There were inspectors and sub-inspectors, deputy area managers and deputy-deputy deputy area managers. They would tell my mother, who had five of us and her dispensary district to run, what they'd like for lunch and what time they'd be back. For a long time my mother put up with it.

My father was involved in what today they'd call rationalisation and given a second book for a few extra shillings and this meant a bigger district and more cycling in wet and windy weather.

What really hurt him, however, was that he found that the new company seemed deadly slow to pay out on the funeral policies and haggled and carped over the most niggling details. In the old days you sent in the death certificate and the policy was paid. Now, it seemed, the new company wanted each claim researched back twenty years or more.

I remember there used to be trouble about the exact age of the insured – anything, it seemed, to hold up the payout. It broke my father's heart to see simple people who had set such store on the "funeral policy" being deprived of quick payments by an army of little mickey-mouse officials, who were more full of their own pompous little bits of titles than they were of the urgent needs of a simple people who knew nothing of the intricacies and jargon of insurance wallahs and for whom the sixpenny or shilling policy was simply money put a-by against the funeral day. Today we would call it bad public relations but the smooth young glib men who went out to small policy-holders had lines of patter and did not talk the same language that my father talked and in consequence were not understood.

The cycling in the wet and wind and rain took its toll on my father: he died before he was fifty and, although he had resigned some years before that because of failing health, there would be many envelopes with small sums which would come for a year after he died, representing the sixpences and shillings and half-crowns he had paid to save policies from lapsing.

Today I can go into some of those villages and though he is dead over twenty years my identity is fixed not by anything I have done in my own right. "You'd be Stephen Healy's son, wouldn't you – if you are half the man your father was, you'll be all right."

It wasn't a sentiment my mother would share: even after his death she would say he had "no cutting" in him and he was "too soft". And she hoped we'd have a "bit more backbone than your father who made a mat of himself for every Tom, Dick and Harry in the district."

I was old enough then to know that my father lived his life the way he lived it and that his nature was a different one to my mother's: she was a woman who had come through a competitive mill and who had to "fight my corner" in New York and never forgot the lessons she learned there.

And yet she never talked of New York and there was little of the sentimental in her. You got mysterious little observations like, "I hope no son of mine ever has a bad word for the Jews", but it was never explained. Or "If it wasn't for America, Jim O'Donnell wouldn't be where he is today."

Jim O'Donnell was in Carracastle, still a big man, and his cart of bonhams, when he had them, was still the best cart of bonhams in the fair of Charlestown. The war was over now and Edward and Bernie had left and there was just Jim and Mary Anne there in the red-tiled house on the hill of Castleduff. The planting of fir-trees I had helped him put down were growing into a thick shelter belt but I saw it now only from the road: we didn't "go up" anymore.

How much of the bad blood was due to Aunt Mary's visit home, with Cousin John, the man who loved them and left them, I can't be sure. Mary and John "couldn't stay abroad in Carracastle" with the cold of the place and Mary Anne wouldn't be able to look after them.

Of course, Jim and Mary Anne expected Aunt Mary and John to stay in the old home: it was only natural – where else would Mary stay but in the place where she was born? Mary Anne was sure she knew that all that was worrying "Nora within" was Mary's trunks and what she had in them. Equally my mother was sure that "all Mary Anne wants is to lay her hands on Mary's trunk."

Sure everyone knew Mary Anne hadn't as much as one linen pillow cover she could put on a pillow – "anything she had was made out of flour bags, God help us."

It went on for weeks before the Yanks arrived and when the train finally came in with them on it, Jim and my mother were on the platform to welcome her and her son.

Mary was everything an American aunt should be: she was an older version of my mother in looks, bigger in physique and fur-coated. Her son John was a roly-poly man with rimless glasses (very expensive) and a real son of Brooklyn.

Aunt Mary would stay with Nora and so the trunks came to our house. They would visit Castleduff.

Cousin John brought me a Bulova watch. Aunt Mary had some clothes in the trunk for us all. Cousin John had the biggest dollar roll I ever saw and he loved beer; he was going to enjoy his first Irish vacation and while his mother and my mother sat at the fire and talked of the old days in Brooklyn, John was enjoying his beer with the boys. John promised that when I had finished my studies he would sponsor me and get me a good job with his brewery company and I could go and stay with "Mom" and himself. That visit put Castleduff more out of bounds for us. Jim had "a nose on him" because Mary and the trunks stayed in Charlestown. "Nora made sure she had the load" and she could keep it and the rest, too, was Mary Anne's verdict.

Poor Mary Anne! But she wasn't that poor. My mother assured Mary Flaherty that old and all as Mary Anne was, she was "hardy" and she'd see Jim down to Carracastle in the box if it was only for spite – and then the Barroes would come into their own on the hill of Castleduff. "And when I think, Mary, how hard we worked in Brooklyn and what we put up with", Mary said you never knew: Jim looked very strong and fit and if Mary Anne was that old when she married . . .

"She's as old as the crows", my mother would explode with impatience, annoyed that her word was doubted. "Still, she hasn't a grey hair in her head", Mary would offer.

"Sure the whole village knows she's been dyeing it for years – did ye notice the plastery way she has it done. Dyed, it is. But tell me, did she have a decent table-cloth itself for ye? God help her but she has no taste – I had to bring out the linen sheets the time M'ma died. She wasn't two years in Castleduff when the sets we sent from Brooklyn were flittered: she let them go red rotten with the dirt . . ."

And so it went, Mary wondering if my mother remembered the time they sent this parcel to M'ma. And the bargains they got from Pat O'Neill when he had his goaty eye on the sisters!

And Mary Anne and Castleduff and the Barroes would be forgotten in a half an hour of remembering how it was in Brooklyn thirty years before. The memories they raked over were from dead days of thirty years before but when the last day was approaching they grew less reminiscent. It was coming once again to the parting time. Cousin John, still fond of his beer, said they'd come more often now that they found it was so pleasant and easy to come. Cousin John went to Castleduff with "Mom" and said it was "real swell" meeting Uncle Jim and he'd have to come to Brooklyn sometime and he kissed Mary Anne until she giggled.

Mary threw her arms around big Jim who looked over her head at a spot on the mantlepiece and said nothing. "All right, Mom: we gotta go now."

And Mary let Jim go and turned and with not a word walked out to the car, looked at what used to be the old house, now used as stabling, dabbed at her eyes and didn't see Jim and Mary Anne wave as she drove away from Castleduff for the last time. It had been almost fifty years since she had left this spot, as a young girl, with the words of my grandmother in her ears as a parting blessing: "Keep your legs and your mouth closed: keep your ears open and send home the ticket for the next one."

Well, she had done that and the next one had been less lucky. Mary could not know then, as she faced back to an America which was now her home and vastly more familiar to her than when she went as a labelled emigrant, that she would end her days on the poverty line on New York, surviving her only son who loved them and left them . . .

CHAPTER EIGHT

The visit of Aunt Mary and Cousin John came in the second half of the 'Forties: it was a good time for Americans because America was then helping to rebuild Europe with Marshall Aid dollars.

Cousin John was rather proud of that and if you had told him that almost a century before the world had ever heard of General Marshall and his aid, the emigrant Irish, Poles, Germans and Italians had invented Marshall Aid and administered it with a ten-cent stamp, he would, like many a native-born American, have been taken aback. The world will never know how much these scared, brave, sometimes ignorant but always loyal emigrants to the New World sent home in dollars and parcels to the old people in the old country. No one will ever know the full extent of their sacrifices and how much they kept hidden from the old people who thought that America was indeed the golden land of opportunity where the streets were truly paved with gold.

Did they not have the dollar cheques at Christmas and Easter and in the autumn from sons and daughters who had left with no skills other than a strong back and a willing pair of hands? Didn't they have the finest of clothes to wear and the lovely linens to send home? And in every letter there was news of John's progress through high school and Junior's progress and Cousin Theresa's scholastic achievements. She would soon be graduating from high school.

High school sounded very grand and the news that cousins were due to graduate seemed very exciting indeed: here at home you just left school and that was that. But it was different in America. We got graduation-day pictures of smart young American cousins and their handsome young beaux. In America a boy-friend or a girl-friend was a beau and something to be admired. In Ireland it was something else again and if it got to your mother's ears that you were taking a girl to the pictures, you might as well prepare for an inquisition and a full read of the poor kid's family tree back for four generations. You could always be sure there was someone in the blood line didn't have a shift to her back until the first of them went to America. And if she had narrow hips, my mother would notice, though I didn't understand what she was talking about.

Aunt Kit was married in Long Island and had a son, Patrick, called Junior, who was one age with me. That meant that when Junior had finished with a suit or shoes or shirts, they were packed into a parcel and sent to Nora for the children. We grew up in linen sailor suits from America and it didn't surprise me that one day there arrived a photograph of Junior, the all-American boy, in his naval ensign's uniform.

Junior's two-toned brogues might be big in the snazzier spots around uptown New York but in downtown Charlestown in the Nineteen Forties it took a lot of courage to walk up Chapel Street in those chocolate-brown-and-cream brogues. Similarly, you looked a bit of a latchiko going to school in Lowpark in hand-me-down American knickerbockers but you had to admit grudgingly in cold weather they were a help. Not to mention those mornings on which Mister Cassidy decided to get some exercise with the cane on the back of your legs.

And every summer there would be photographs or winter letters from Florida where Uncle Pat and Aunt Kit would be "vacationing". And, as always, they expressed the hope that they'd make the trip home next year.

My mother was certain that after John and Aunt Mary had made the trip that Uncle Pat and Aunt Kit would surely come, for Uncle Pat was very wealthy indeed (my mother was sure of that). "He had his money made before I came home", she'd say with a conviction which implied that if she wanted to talk she could say a lot more.

It was in one of the summer photographs of Kit's family that my mother noticed that young Cousin Theresa had an odd way of standing. In the Christmas photograph she thought she noticed it again and the following summer she was sure that "that child isn't developing right". She wrote to Aunt Kit and asked her.

Aunt Kit said something about her having a fall from her pony and hurting her hip but the doctors said it was all right. My mother was sure it wasn't and went back to her photos and wrote again to Kit . . .

When my father died, Uncle Pat cabled the funeral expenses and now the cheques at Christmas and Easter were more generous from Uncle Pat.

Aunt Mary never forgot either and, with Cousin John, sent the regular fifty dollars at Easter and a hundred dollars at Christmas. Uncle Jim got the same from Mary and Pat O'Neill.

Aunt Mary's letters in the 'Fifties were full of news. John had done so well with the brewery that he had bought his own tavern in Brooklyn and he was in business for himself . . .

Aunt Kit had the same news too; she supposed we had heard that John was opening a tavern and she didn't know how well he'd do, but they were all hoping for the best for him: he had a good stand . . . Theresa was in hospital with her hip but she was hopeful she'd be out soon . . . Junior was engaged to be married and she was glad to hear that John had gone on for journalism and Kevin was thinking of the priesthood, and she knew Pat would help out . . . There was still no sign of Cousin John getting married . . . maybe now with the tavern, he'd meet someone.

And my mother would shake her head at Kit's ambitions for John and remark again that he was the wise one for he loved them and left them and looked after his mother like any good son should.

There had been a thaw in the relationship with Uncle Jim in Carracastle with the death of my father but this time I was already in Dublin and the world of Carracastle, like the world of American aunts and uncles and cousins, was slipping more and more into the background.

When I visited home now, the American letters were kept for me to read but my interests had changed. I would get to America yet and see Mary and John again and go to Kohr Road, Long Island, to see

63

Kit and Uncle Pat and Cousin Junior and his wife, and cousin Theresa who was, once again, out of hospital.

But I would marry first and have my own family started, and I would go with the old Irish dream that America was indeed the land of opportunity and easy meat for a sharp young Irishman who had good connections in New York – with a cousin who owned a tavern and an uncle who was a wheel in the Democratic Party on Long Island and who owned a hunk of real estate in downtown Brooklyn.

I did finally make it on a cold February day in 1957 and with a one-way ticket to New York and pier 86.

There was no Aunt Mary or Cousin John waiting at the Customs exit and I wouldn't have known Uncle Pat or Aunt Kit, never having met them.

Well, I thought, it doesn't matter for I did have some officials from the US State Department who had been detailed off to meet me and take me to my hotel. There had been a tugboat strike and maybe they had figured I wouldn't get in for another day or two. Well tomorrow there would be the big reunion in 1070 Nostrand Avenue, Brooklyn, or in Kohr Road, Kings Park, Long Island.

I got the telephone directories out and searched up Flaherty, Brooklyn, and O'Neill, Long Island, and put in my calls. Wouldn't they be surprised – Nora's son had made it to New York under his own steam!

Nora O'Donnell

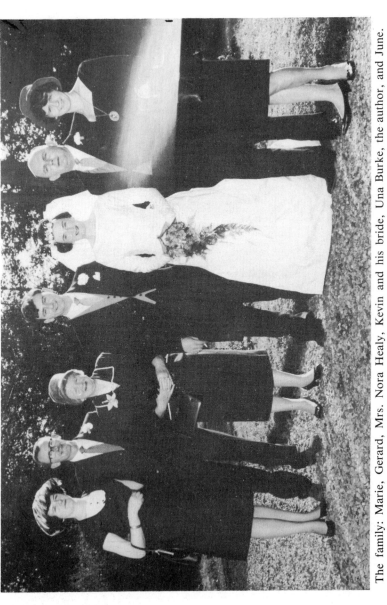

The family: Marie, Gerard, Mrs. Nora Healy, Kevin and his bride, Una Burke, the author, and June.

Left to right: Fr. Joe O'Neill; his father, Uncle Patrick O'Neill; Una Healy; her husband, Kevin; Aunt Catherine (Kit) O'Neill; Nora O'Donnell (Healy). Seated: Cousin Theresa O'Neill.

St. Patrick's Day Parade down Fifth Avenue, 17 March 1941. On the exteme
left is John Flaherty and third from the left is attorney Paul O'Dwyer who
would later help both John and his mother Mary in less happy times.

Uncle Pat O'Neill congratulates Kevin Healy after his marriage.

CHAPTER NINE

We all have our moments in life. It is one of life's great gifts to be able to savour them as they are happening. It is the first time, as a boy, you ride a man's bicycle from the saddle . . . it is coming from an inland town and never having seen a boat, much less sat in one, rowing up to Menlo Castle . . . it is seeing your first words in print . . .

Or it is walking into Times Square, New York, and feeling utterly and perfectly at home even though you are a long way from Charlestown, County Mayo.

It nearly didn't happen in 1957. Some months earlier the American Embassy had scouted the idea of my being an exchange writer. I said that if the opportunity arose I'd be quite happy to pay my international travel expenses (these were normally paid). The idea seemed to fall through, so the money I had earmarked was spent on the home. Then came an offer from the Embassy: could I travel in two weeks time? The American dream was a reality if only I could raise the transatlantic fare. I was then working in Burgh Quay with *The Irish Press* and it had a most prudent management in money matters. The best the management could do for me was to give me leave of absence for six months . . . that was also the time when a bank porter could cut you **dead** because banks didn't want to know you unless you had money.

I was chewing over the problem with some of the lads in the newsroom who knew my determination to make it one way or the other. Afterwards Ted Nealon, a neighbour from Aclare, who was then working with me in the *Press*, followed me quietly downstairs and asked me what I needed. "The price of a single ticket will do me,

Ted, because I'll hitch a ride home if I have to'', I said. He gave me £100 out of savings he had. (Incidentally, neck or ambition, or whatever you want to call it, is one great asset: I did, in fact, hitch a lift home. More correctly I got the US Military Air Transport Service, known as MATS, to drop me off in Scotland.)

So you can understand why I felt good the day I drove up Fifth Avenue, New York, firing questions about New York city politicians at my State Department hosts who were to wonder at the intimate knowledge I seemed to have: they couldn't know that an old boy of St. Nathy's, and a neighbour's child, had conquered this city and ruled it not many years before. We wore the campaign badges for Bill O'Dwyer in Nathy's and we got a free day in the college when the news was announced he had been elected Mayor of New York. From that day on, New York politics became one of my favourite studies.

To be sure New York wasn't the same city to which Aunt Mary, Aunt Anna, Aunt Kit and my mother, came in the first decade of the century. I had come to New York in 1957 after almost a decade of newspapering which had taken me to a large town like Ballina, on to Dublin and, later, to most of the major cities of the Continent, including East Berlin behind the Iron Curtain. I had some experience of cities and city life, and I was mature to some degree or other.

But what must it have been like for Aunt Mary, the first to go, with a tag in her lapel, from a small thatched cottage on the side of a hill in Carracastle, never having seen a town but what she passed on her way to Queenstown, and to arrive in this polyglot city of New York a few weeks later? How did she survive? How did she prosper? For prosper she did: hadn't she come home in her furs and rich clothes? Hadn't John done well, running his own tavern? Weren't they able to send my mother the cheques for fifty and a hundred dollars regularly? Wasn't Aunt Kit on Long Island with her big house and Uncle Pat running his business in Brooklyn? He, too, was an emigrant from Donegal who got little education and was now an important ranking man in the Democratic Party on Long Island.

Questions like these didn't occur to me in 1957 because you took the American dream for granted and because, I suppose, I was too busy savouring my own accomplishment at having actually made it to Times Square.

Part of that savouring would be when I actually stood on the stoop (for some reason or other I thought Aunt Mary's house would have a stoop) of 1070 Nostrand Avenue, Brooklyn, when Aunt Mary would open the door and, with Cousin John, greet me with all the excitement with which we had greeted them over ten years before.

I caught a train to Brooklyn and revelled in the placenames as they came up: you could almost hear the husky smokey voice of Ella Fitzgerald singing them as she did in "Manhattan".

I looked twice at 1070 Nostrand Avenue and for the first time I wondered if I had made a mistake. Years of posting air-mail letters to this address had led me to think of it as a house with a stoop, set in a nice residential area. But this was a shopping street, something like Richmond Street in Dublin: old and lived in. A friendly street really. 1070 was a door with several bells on it. I was still looking when the door opened and a wizened little woman said truculently:

"You want-a someone, mistah?"

"I'm looking for a Mrs. Flaherty."

She made an Italian noise and said something about two flights up, stepped back to let me pass her and, as I started up the stairs, shouted something after me before banging the door closed.

Two flights up I knocked. The old woman in the housecoat who opened the door was an older version of my mother: there could be no mistaking Aunt Mary and her lovely clear soft skin. She just threw her arms around me and wept . . .

It was a full minute before she called Cousin John. Although it was midday, he was still in bed.

"Come and see who's here from Ireland."

Cousin John came, limping. He was bloated now, and seemed older than his years but still with that virgin-boy look to him.

Gee, it was swell seeing me again . . .

"Momma, do we have a beer in the ice-box?"

I say not to bother, I don't drink and John says, Hell, he'd like one anyway and Momma, who is wiping the last of the tears from her eyes, says with an infinite sadness, "So early in the day you should want a beer?"

I remember the phrase because it has a Jewish construction and at that particular moment Aunt Mary seemed to be the typical down-trodden Jewish mother who knows life offers nothing but misfortunes but God is good yet and you still ask a question even though you know the answer. John opens the ice-box. It has three tins of beer, a carton of milk, and nothing else.

Nothing else.

I have brought two canisters of Irish tea with me and some Irish linen table cloths and napkins. I make a joke as John opens the beer. "Here, Aunt Mary, we'll have a few cups of strong Irish tea."

From halfway down the stairs comes an Italian voice, shouting I dont know what. Mary smiles a little:

"The wops."

John is talking, half answering the shrill voice outside but Mary is already boiling the kettle in the small kitchen off the two-roomed flat, calling to John to get dressed and go down to the store to get some things.

John says his foot is giving him hell, switches on the television set and sinks back in one of the two armchairs with his beer.

I tell Mary I'll go down. I know where the delicatessen is because I passed it coming down the block.

I was on a budget of twelve dollars a day, out of which I still had to send home the equivalent of my week's wages in *The Irish Press*, so I had to be careful of my spending. She went to get some change but I told her not to worry, I'd get it.

I brought back a bag of groceries. It took the bare look off the ice-box. I had six cans of beer for Cousin John.

We ate and Cousin John had to go to a hospital clinic with his foot. Mary advised him to be careful and as he went down the stairs the Italian voice opened up again and did not stop until the door banged behind him. Mary and myself spent the afternoon drinking tea and more tea and talking.

She cried a lot first and then, slowly, the worst of her story over, she

68

smiled a bit more and then it was my turn to weep with rage at what she had gone through and the facade she had put up rather than admit that the American dream was now for her an illusion.

Aunt Mary was the first of my mother's family to come to America. She had come with a label on her and had passed through Ellis Island where she got the first crude mark of approval on her black coat: a chalked "F" which said she was "fit" and could enter the Land of the Free.

She had left Castleduff in the spring of her life and of the year. M'ma's parting words were plain enough to her. She had come to some of her own and they met her: they were relations of my grand-people who had come earlier and had settled and were prospering. They were prospering indeed to the point where they wanted an Irish help and Mary, with no education beyond what she got in Cloonfane school, went into the kitchen.

She wasn't the first Irish biddy in New York but she would be the last of that family. She had her board and she made do with the cast-off clothes of the house. At the Catholic church on Sunday you were expected to put a whole dollar in the plate, for there were schools and churches to be built by and for the Irish Catholics. I have never gone into New York's cathedral without thinking of the Mary O'Donnells of the old world and their sweated dollars which went into the building of it. But they did it.

Slowly, too, she gathered the dollars for the one-way ticket for her younger sister, Anna.

She was a red-haired Irish colleen, a typical Irish beauty and she, too, had just left school. A Jewish doctor, who had come to attend in the house in which Mary worked, noticed how neat Mary was in her housework (and probably noted her beauty, too, for she was a very attractive woman, even in her old age) and inquired where she came from and how many she had in her family in the old country.

It was around the time Anna was on the Atlantic on her way and Mary said proudly that her sister was joining her. Did she have a job? No, but Mary was hoping to "place her in service". The Jewish doctor said he would like to see her when she came. He left his address. When

69

Anna arrived, she and Mary presented themselves at the Brooklyn home of the Jewish doctor and, immediately Anna had a job. She, too, had parted with M'ma with the same old blessing. Anna and her red-haired beauty and alertness won that Jewish doctor's admiration and he gave her the ambition to be a nurse: if she could go to night school for a time, he would see about placing her in the hospital where he worked.

He was as good as his word so that when Anna left his service she had already the price of the passage for Nora, my mother, who was to take her place in the Jewish household.

My grandmother never changed the parting blessing: my mother, too, was told what to do and to send home the passage money for Kitty. Anna had neglected to tell M'ma to be sure to get a reference from the schoolmaster in Cloonfane saying she had reached high school standard so that Nora, too, could enter night classes. My mother had "awful trouble" later trying to make the schoolmaster at home understand what was wanted of him.

She took Anna's place in the doctor's home, her place in night school and her place as a student nurse, and sent home the passage money for Kitty who, in turn, took my mother's place in the kitchen, the schoolroom and the hospital.

M'ma's parting words to Kitty were a bit different: "You are the last of them now. Remember what to do: keep your mouth and your legs closed, keep you ears open; tell the others that between ye, ye'll send home the slates."

Grandma never cried at the station in Charlestown when she sent them away. She never went that far on the road. She turned at the main tar road and it was on the boreen leading to her own cottage that she would be a mother by allowing herself the luxury of weeping.

It was Kitty who told me she had gone with her in the pony and trap to see my mother off and "she cried her 'nough" between the bottom of the boreen and the cottage at the top of the hill: her eyes would be dry by the time she reached "the street" in front of the cottage and she'd be calling out jobs to Jim and Michael even before she got out of the trap.

Mary married a fireman called Flaherty, a Galwayman; they rented a house, and, with her three sisters now in New York and either qualified nurses or on the way to being qualified, she set a flat in it for them. Mary's "catch" was regarded as a good one: he had a job with "the city" and it was pensionable. A fireman or a policeman was regarded as a good catch for a kitchen biddy because he offered the security of working for "the city": it was the equivalent in Ireland later of a civil service job.

But like many an Irishman who "worked for the city", he had a fondness for the drink and one night he met with a fatal accident. Mary was left a widow very early with the one gosling son who was to be spoiled and pampered by his mother and three vivacious aunts. "We had good times and bad times", said Aunt Mary, "but we had fun in the old days."

I remember my mother saying to me one time in one of the very rare occasions in which she talked of America: "No child of mine should ever say anything against the Jews for they put many a penny my way in my time." One other fragment was that most of the pennies were made during the Great Flu of 1919 when thousands died in New York: my mother once said that she became so accustomed to the odour of death that, as soon as she crossed the threshold of a sick house, she knew just how long it would be before death came.

Aunt Mary, on that February day in 1957, filled out the portrait of my mother in those days and she was indeed in some respects a different woman to the stern, driving woman I grew up with.

"Yes, she could smell the death in those days. You see the three girls had a great 'in' with the Jewish doctors in the hospital in those days: they were all very good-looking girls and Anna and Kitty had this lovely red colleen hair. And, of course, when Jewish people in this section went down with the flu and called for attention, the Jewish doctors would go to them and if someone had to have a nurse they always put in a word for the Nurse O'Donnells – Anna, Nora and Kitty.

"Nora wouldn't be in a house with a Jewish person two minutes before she knew, to the hour, when that poor person would close her eyes for the last time. She used to ring the nurses' bureau they had here that time and tell them that she'd be available for a fresh call at such a time. She would give herself time to lay out the corpse and she'd be back at the flat sitting by the phone waiting for another call, and she was never out in her timing that I know of.''

But even the Nurse O'Donnells were vulnerable and Anna was in as much demand as my mother.

Anna was a worrier in those days, Aunt Mary remembered, and her biggest worry of all was her dough-boy sweetheart: he had enlisted with the American army and had gone to Europe. ''She lived for his letters from Europe and, if they didn't come on time, she imagined all sorts of things happening to him in the Great War. She was stone daft about the lad – another Galway fellow – I think she met him when he came to see my man. At any rate, when they called the Armistice he was still alive but for some reason or other his regiment had to stay on in France after the war was over. The flu was raging in New York when his ship left for America and Anna, like the rest of them, was run off her feet, night and day, attending to dying people. She didn't mind – her man was on his way home and they were to get married and the flu was a godsend in a way to her because she was piling up the dollars – and Anna was making great money because she was getting the richest Jewish houses. What she couldn't handle, she put on to Nora, your mother. Anna knew which ones were rich and which were, well, just comfortable. When she caught the flu herself, Nora took over her calls. And then Nora walked in one night and said she got the death smell when she opened the door . . . Poor Anna was dead – whipped away – that morning at two . . .''

Her dough-boy sweetheart arrived a week after they buried her in Brooklyn. He came to visit Anna to find the news before him. He took the Irish solution to tragedy, drank himself insensible in some saloon and was mugged for his demobilisation bank-roll. They fished his body from the East River three days afterwards, minus a hand. By the time the police inquest was over and the formalities dispensed with, the body had been coffined for burial; waterfront policemen, dredging for another body, fished up the missing hand, put it in a box and it was placed on the coffin. He had no family in Brooklyn to say where he might be buried, so the sisters decided he would have a grave beside the fresh grave of the girl he had planned to marry.

"The last of the flowers hadn't withered on Anna's grave the day we put him down beside her . . . They were hard days but we came through them to better times, thank God and his Blessed Mother."

And we drank more tea while Aunt Mary remembered the better times . . .

CHAPTER TEN

America in the post war years of the Nineteen Twenties is remembered now in songs of the period as a swinging place. It is the America of the flapper girls, the elegant lounge lizards, the vamps who danced the Black-Bottom and, in New York, the gay young things felt they were letting the side down if they beat the milkman to the dawn doorstep after a night on the tiles. I couldn't see my mother quite making that scene, or Aunt Mary either, for that matter.

My mother, I imagined, would frown at the flapper era girls and would want to know where their dignity was, flaunting themselves like that. She was a very good step-dancer and had small nimble feet but there was a world of difference between doing a slip jig and dancing the Charleston.

"She did the two of them in her day and she didn't lack for boyfriends", said Aunt Mary, smiling again as she remembered. "She wasn't above flirting when it suited her: she could glad-eye a man as good as the next, especially if she was looking for a bargain in something. And she was always on the look-out for a bargain, whether it was a sailor suit for John or a pair of linen sheets to put in a parcel home to M'ma in Castleduff. Sure she nearly drove Pat O'Neill wild in those days – herself and Kit. Pat had the store down there on Fifth Avenue – you'll see it, I'm sure – and Kit and Nora used go down to hunt a bargain when they'd be making up a parcel for Castleduff."

"My mother used to say Uncle Pat always had a goaty eye – was that right?"

Mary laughed.

"She never said anything else about him – and she was the same girl

74

who knew it and made the good use of it. She got bargains out of Pat O'Neill that no one else got and some of the stuff she sent home to Castleduff, and was there when we went home, came from Fifth Avenue and Nora had it for next to nothing. Pat was daft about her even then."

"How do you mean 'even then'?"

"Well his first wife was alive though she was dying slowly."

"I thought Auntie Kit was his first wife."

"No, no. Kitty was his second wife. He met her when herself and Nora used to go in to get some bargains in the pawn office. Pat owned the pawn office: well, I can't remember whether he owned it then or whether it was the time of the partnership. There was a man called Kelly who owned it originally and he brought Pat in as a young lad. Pat was from Donegal and his first job was putting down the pavement setts on the streets here in Brooklyn. He used to make ten dollars a week, wet or dry. He struck up with this Kelly man someway and I often heard him say Kelly offered him eight dollars a week to come and work in the store. That was two dollars a week less than what he was making with the city but Pat thought there might be more of a future behind the counter than on the streets, and he took it.

"Some of his mates said he was making a mistake to change his job for less because in those days you only changed a job if you got more but Pat held it was better to be behind the counter and he took the job.

"At the time I'm talking about, when Nora and Kit were going into him, he owned part of the store with this Kelly man and he was very comfortable. Nora and Kit knew well he was married because Nora wouldn't stop until she found out a thing like that but they didn't let on to Pat. And he had a goaty eye, surely, but who'd blame him with that pair . . . They had the best of things, suits for Jim and D'da . . . an astrakhan coat for M'ma . . . the best of linens and they'd get them for half nothing. A parcel never went to Castleduff but most of it came from Pat O'Neill's on Fifth Avenue.

"His wife was a long time dying, the poor thing, and Nora had gone home by this time. That'd be about '27 or '28. Pat was dead struck on her and, although she was gone home to Ireland, he was determined to follow her. Kit used to go into him after Nora left, for she had to send home things, and one day he showed a ticket he had just bought from the shipping line: he was going home to ask Nora to marry him.

"Kit wouldn't believe him until he showed her the sailing ticket and, there and then, she said to him it was far he was going for an O'Donnell woman and one of them nearer to him than Ireland.

"Pat looked at her and asked her if he understood her all right and what she was saying. Kit told him, as bold as you like, he didn't have to go to Ireland for an O'Donnell.

"Pat wasn't long changing his mind: he went out and bought another ticket and the two of them went home to Ireland on the one boat and made a honeymoon of it. Nora was going with your father that time and I remember well when Kit came back from Ireland, she said Nora had a very nice man who was a great dancer – he waltzed her off her feet and our Kit loved a waltz. Poor Pat wasn't much of a fist at the dancing and, of course, he was a bit older than Kit. Kit loved the dancing in her day but her dancing days ended when she married Pat O'Neill . . ."

I knew from the way she let the sentence trail off that there was more to the story than Kitty O'Donnell having to buckle down to married life.

"How is Aunt Kit?"

"She has a good man: Pat has been a good husband to her."

"She's in good health?" This was probing, for I was sensing that there was something in the background and Mary was reluctant to say what it was.

"She comes in and out. John and herself don't always see eye to eye because she feels John let Pat down. John and Pat don't pull too well ever since the time John bought the tavern."

The water was getting deeper now and the face which had seemed so young as she talked of the days of Nora and Kitty and Pat of the goaty eye seemed shadowed with an old hurt. It was a sort of bafflement, as if even yet she didn't fully understand what had really happened.

She was looking into the bottom of the cup so that you'd think the leaves held some of the answers or would tell her where to begin to understand.

Then she said, very slowly: "I don't know, John agradh . . . all the things that happened to us . . . first the tavern . . . then the diabetes and now the leg and poor John can't work . . . there is nothing coming in except what Kit sends me or Pat sends me in her name because Kit hasn't the handling of anything anymore . . ."

I waited, without understanding, and then said: "But you told me she's comfortable."

"There isn't a thing on the wide earthly world she wants for but Pat will bring it and have it for her but he has to do all the handling of the money. But she's happy enough now to have it that way . . . Kit had her own troubles, God help her – she still has them and she'll have them to the grave."

It did not seem possible that this lovely young girl, whose vivacious smiling photograph was on the mantlepiece of the sittingroom at home, could ever have troubles. In all the years of reading her letters in Carracastle and Charlestown there was no hint of any troubles of any kind. The cheques and the size of them and the regularity of them all bore witness to the legend of the Great American Dream coming true for her and her man.

Hadn't Uncle Pat ridden out the Depression years and hadn't he made a second journey home with Kit and their son Junior, and was able to do it when America had as its new national anthem, the song: "Buddy, can you spare a dime?"

The pictures on the mantlepiece 3,000 miles away at home in Charlestown were as clear before my eyes: Kit in her furs . . . Kit in a head-and-shoulders study, peach-skinned and eyes sparkling with flirtatious devilment. Kit's son Junior, smart in his Navy hat and clean-shaven chin, the very picture of the American success story. It was true that we did not have studio pictures of Theresa but we did have the ordinary snapshots showing her smiling beside a swimming pool or with her thoroughbred dalmatians.

Very gently I asked: "What about the tavern?"

She lifted her head and her two blue eyes, half filmed at the remembering: "It's gone, agradh . . . a neighbour of yours from home has it now . . ."

"What happened?"

"Everything happened . . . everything . . . and he was doing so well in Schaeffer's. Everyone knew him and he knew everyone. They all said that when he opened his own business . . ."

She looked at the tea leaves again.

"John says it was the Mafia. The wops. They wanted him to do this and do that. He had to put in this kind of fitting and that kind of fitting and they'd supply it. I don't know, I don't undersand these things . . . That's why he's always fighting with that strap downstairs: she's a wop. John says it was the Mafia that put him out of business – he can't stand Italians since.

"And then there was the row with Pat O'Neill. Pat put money into the tavern. I don't know how much because Pat has a habit of being close when he's dealing with money. He never told me and Kit doesn't know, but I know he backed John in it and felt let down. He used to come to visit me but John and himself could hardly meet after the tavern went and Pat stopped coming. Kit comes whenever she leaves the Island."

"Did John lose everything: I mean, surely he got something when he sold it?"

"It had to be sold to meet the debts and even that wasn't enough. Pat O'Neill never got his money out of it, whether it was big or little, I don't know."

"Could he not go back to the brewery?"

"Well he has this diabetes and the leg and he is as you see him, and that's all he has and that's all I have except I have my health, thank God, and Kit and Pat have kept this roof over us so we could be worse. Paul O'Dwyer is trying to get something from the city for John. He's the lawyer up at O'Dwyer and Bernsteins and John told him he hurt his foot coming out of City Hall. He has a claim in for John and he may get something: he can't look for work until the claim is settled one way or another and God knows how long that'll take.

I have welfare and that keeps a bit on the table. John sits here during the day and all he can do is drink beer and the doctor told him he shouldn't, but what else is there, John agradh?"

And slowly she lifted those blue eyes and they trembled as she said: "And that's how we are and that's how you find us." The tears did not come and she did not break the gaze for there was no self-pity in Mary Flaherty: the gaze was unflinching and it asked me to accept things as they were and to undersand that she had accepted these things, too.

"How long has it been like this, Aunt Mary?"

"A long time, John agradh, a long time."

"But the letters and the cheques . . ."

The rest of that sentence never came and I saw the smile on her face before it went blurred in front of me and a terrible frustration choked me. I was trying to find words to explain to her that what she had done was monstrous but I could only hear her saying: "Two dollars a week from Easter to Christmas: it wasn't a lot but it stopped Nora and Jim from worrying. They didn't have to know: they had enough troubles of their own."

"But Aunt Mary: you were home in '47. You saw our house. You saw Jim's house. You saw the land. You knew we were comfortable. You knew we were better off than you and John were – why did you do it? Why?"

"I always did it and if I didn't Nora's robin wouldn't sing on the bush."

Even yet the same phrase jumps to my lips: that stupid bastardin' robin.

When she and John had been home, she noticed a robin singing on a small bush outside our back door. My mother explained to her that she always knew when the Brooklyn letter was coming because the robin sang for two days before it was delivered. "Always", said my mother, "I know the day it is due because that robin nearly bursts himself singing and he comes right up to the back door."

Now it is true that my mother had a great faith in that robin. There was one year the robin didn't sing and, we thought my mother hadn't noticed it, she told us there must be something wrong with Mary because her robin wasn't singing.

We told her it was nonsense – robins didn't know what happened in America: they sang because they were staking out their territory, warning other robins off. I got the back of her left hand across the mouth for such heresies – how dare I cross her when she knew there was something wrong with Mary?

Call it a coincidence or anything you like: that was the year that Mary's letter and her fifty dollar cheque didn't come until the second week of the New Year.

John had had an accident and, since he did most of the letter writing and signed the money order, the Brooklyn letter had to wait until he recovered. The robin was right. My mother had believed so implicitly in the robin that she wrote a quick letter to Mary two days before Christmas (which would be about a week after the Brooklyn letter would normally have arrived) to ask if she was well and all right?

When, in the New Year, John's letter and money-order arrived belatedly, my mother wrote back to thank them and explained why she had been so worried before Christmas: Mary's robin wasn't singing and she knew something was wrong.

Mary had remembered the robin in all these years of existing on the poverty line in Brooklyn, New York, and from her social security cheque she would squirrel away two dollars, because it was a short gap between Christmas and Easter, to make an Easter cheque and a dollar a week from Easter to Thanksgiving so that Jim and Nora would believe that as with Kit, the American dream was still holding up for Mary Flaherty and her one gosling son who loved them and left them.

"Nora was good to me in the years when my man died and I didn't really know how it was with her when poor Stephen went. She had five mouths to fill . . ."

And then that lovely face broke into a warm smile: "Is Nora's robin still singing on the bush?"

"Nora's robin is called Mary's robin at home and Mary's robin sings louder than ever."

"That's good . . . that's good . . . that's good."

80

She was happy then and she made another pot of tea, smiling to herself at the stove. God rest her generous dust and the thousands of
great people like her who went from our country and shared what they
had and made, down to the social welfare dollar.

CHAPTER ELEVEN

The actual shop floor space was small in Kelly and O'Neill's pawnshop on Fifth Avenue, New York, and the man behind the counter didn't look like Pat O'Neill. I told him I wanted to see Mr. O'Neill. He went into an office and there was no mistaking the blue-suited man with the gold watch chain who came behind him and was already eyeing me.

"You have to be my nephew from Ireland." We shook hands, very warmly. He had indeed a goaty eye when he looked at you sideways but the eyes could smile. Not that hearty smile of the middle-aged man for there was a reserve about him. I tried to imagine him as a young lad from Donegal laying setts on the streets of Brooklyn but I could not place him in any other setting than the one I was to see him in – a blue-suited, quiet-spoken businessman who said little.

He looked at me a little critically; he seemed to be interested in my long Donegal tweed overcoat and asked me if I cared to take it off. He looked at my new suit (for I had bought a whole new rig-out for the American trip) and made a mental note.

He would be going out to Long Island in an hour: did I have any shopping to do? I said I didn't think so but there were a few things I might need later on.

Did I have a supply of shirts? There was a good store across the street.

He pulled a billfold from his pocket, took out a note and asked the man in the shop to take me across to the haberdashery to see some shirts. He was to "look after me" and see I got what I wanted. I bought three of those woollen lumbershirts they advertised in full pages in the *Saturday Evening Post* and returned in time to catch the train to Long Island. When I had rung Aunt Kit on the phone two days before and asked her if I'd take a cab to Kings Park, she laughed. In my pattern of New York, Long Island was about as far out as Dun Laoghaire was from Dublin City centre: after all Uncle Pat commuted to work every morning and I figured that eight miles was the maximum anyone commuted.

She was, she told me, about forty-five or fifty miles from Grand Central and the train took an hour. That was almost as far out as Mullingar from Dublin and when I said that, the amazement must have registered over the phone.

"Why not catch the next train out?"

"Hold on a minute, Aunt Kit – at home I want half a day's notice before I start for Mullingar. I'll leave it tonight and I'll call you tomorrow."

I did, but it was to tell her I was spending the day with Aunt Mary and would visit her the next day. Why didn't I pick up Uncle Pat in Fifth Avenue and come on out with him?

And now we were on our way. Pat had purchased an evening paper and settled back to read; I was content to watch the landscape slip by. I was travelling with an open mind after the experience in Brooklyn but, so far, things seemed to have been real enough. The pawnshop, for instance, although it had little counter space, had stretched way back and Uncle Pat had taken me through it. It was like nothing I had seen in Dublin and clearly the traffic came from a very different social stratum. One room was a stockroom for a small arsenal of guns and rifles, many of them sporting guns with telescopic sights. Another strongroom was used to keep silver plate and jewellery.

Pat knew I was making mental comparisons with the traffic at home and the Monday morning rush to pawn the blankets. It was, he explained, a different sort of trade here. Many items like mink coats belonged to comfortable women who had a storage problem in the hot weather dogdays: many of them solved it by putting the coats in hock.

At the Kings Park station Uncle Pat took out the keys of his Ford car, a long, low, sleek new model where everything was fingertip controlled. He explained that he drove to the local station and parked his car there all day, picking it up each evening to drive home. That was almost a speech for Uncle Pat.

We turned into Kohr Road but again the mental picture I had formed was wrong. Instead of the suburban row I had expected, each house stood on its own grounds and some so far back as to be screened from the road: only mail boxes betrayed the presence of a home.

Pat O'Neill's house was approached by a short drive. On the entrance was a legend, in Gaelic script: *Ár Caisleán Mór.*[14] The legend and the reality matched: it was a big stone-faced house, set in parkland. Spaciousness is the word I kept thinking of all that day and the next. In the lounge the oil paintings ran from polished floor to ceiling.

"Catherine", Uncle Pat called out. "Come meet your nephew from Ireland."

Catherine came.

She was heavy-featured and flabby. Her face was flabby; her figure was flabby; her walk was flabby; her hand was flabby. Only in her hair, as in her eyes when she smiled later, was there a resemblance of the beautiful red-headed Kitty O'Donnell whose lovely features are still etched on my mind's eye to this day.

She had run to flesh and her dress was too tight. She kissed me and we went into the living room. Cousin Theresa was sitting in a wheelchair, her mother's daughter.

Uncle Pat went to a sideboard, unlocked it, and asked me if I'd like a highball before we ate? I explained to him that I was a Pioneer and didn't take intoxicating liquor.

That seemed to surprise him. "I thought all good newspapermen drank."

He poured one for himself, recorked the bottle and put it back in the sideboard, locking it carefully. Would I drink a Coke? Catherine got the Coke. Uncle Pat welcomed me formally to their big castle and asked Catherine what there was for dinner.

He finished his drink and, while Catherine busied herself with the dinner, Uncle Pat took me right through the house. It was sumptuously furnished and spacious. The grounds were as spacious. He

14. Our Big Castle.

84

kept and killed his own fowl and some game birds. He showed me the first deep-freeze I had ever seen and explained how he and a neighbour purchased their cattle and had them killed and dressed and put down, with the turkeys and chickens, in the deep-freeze.

It was all matter-of-fact: as if it were something you should know about the running and management of a house like this. I admired the oil paintings but Uncle Pat volunteered no information about them. They were there and he accepted them as part of the furniture. There was nothing, it seemed, to be explained about them: they were self-explanatory. You didn't explain them any more than you explained the fittings in the bathroom: it was enough to know where they were located in case you wanted to use them.

The meal was almost formal. Uncle Pat ate away with a steady appetite, picking here and rejecting there. He said little. A routine question to Theresa who answered as routinely. Another to Catherine and Catherine replied like a woman going through the motions.

I waited for my cue and it seemed a long time coming. Finally Catherine asked how my mother was and I suppose I made something of a speech.

Uncle Pat munched away as if to a time-schedule. Catherine kept her eyes on the plate as I talked and told her what each of us at home had been doing. I wasn't getting through when Uncle Pat asked if Catherine was ready for coffee; it seemed a good time to end the recital.

After coffee, Uncle Pat switched on the television and wanted to know did we have television yet in Ireland? I said no. Then I'd probably enjoy this. We had baseball from somewhere in the South, or rather a report of some of the teams working in the sunshine of Florida getting ready for the new season. We had Jackie Gleason and Phil Silvers but Catherine and Theresa did not think them very funny. At ten Theresa was taken to bed. At eleven Uncle Pat switched off the television, said we should all turn in and showed me to my room. Catherine came down to see that I was comfortable and kissed me good-night.

We looked at each other, long and intent. There was an old and

85

deep and tired sadness in her eyes which she did not try to hide. Finally she said: "You are Stephen's son and for that you will always be welcome: he was a grand boy." And somewhere in the back of those eyes there was the faintest hint of the eyes on the mantlepiece at home. Kit's eyes. She said goodnight and left . . .

Unlike Mary, Kit seemed to have no time for memories; it was as if she had been drained of all memories or just didn't want to remember. She couldn't even remember the studio photographs she had sent home. She seemed to be surprised that she was ever photographed in an off-the-shoulder evening dress.

She talked a little of M'ma and remembered the roses under the thatch and the well at the bottom of the Hill. And coming home in the pony and trap after my mother left for America. She remembered the trip home to Ireland after the Wall Street Crash.

"Stephen – your father – was a lovely boy. My, how he could waltz! You were only a baby then . . ." And the warmth which had crept into her eyes and voice faded again and she did not want to remember anymore.

I talked of how it was in Castleduff now, the new house, the old house in stablings except the dairy was where it always was, in the old parlour. Mary Anne had made a new gairdín[15] behind where Dolly the horse used to be stabled. She had grown peas and strawberries in it – strawberries, imagine, in Castleduff! I remembered one evening when Grandma took a brown paper sugar-bag and raided the strawberry patch behind Mary Anne's back and gave me the full of it to bring into Charlestown "and don't let on where you got them". I set off on the bicycle on a hot summer's twilight for home, clutching the precious strawberries. I got to Cloonfane when a thunderburst opened the skies. The torrential rain soaked the paper bag and the bottom burst: the strawberries fell out in a praiseach[16] on the road. I gathered up what I could and ran for the shelter of the lone hawthorn bush beyond Bob Red's.

"That's not still there, is it?"

15. Garden.
16. Bruised mess.

"You know the one I mean – on the right-hand side as you go into the town, just beyond Bob Red's."

"Of course I remember it – it's the only bush on that stretch of the road. It's nice to think it's still there . . . but why didn't you go back to Bob Red's house?"

As a matter of fact I did in the end. Indeed, I was driven against a fear to go back to it when the rain kept on coming down in sheets. Bob Red's mother was supposed to be a bit odd and it was a house you hurried by when going to or from Carracastle. She always shouted, it seemed, when she wanted to say anything. She was probably hard of hearing but between that and her style of dressing she was something of a witch in my child's memory. But now there was nothing for it but to go back to that fearful house.

The level of the house was below the road and it was a thatched cottage. Bob Red seemed twice the height of the kitchen door and it was always open. I went in trembling, as much from fear as from the wetting. It was appropriately gloomy and Bob was above at the fire, a heap of clothes in front of it and, from the heap, he was feeding the flames.

"Hullo there – come in outa that rain", he shouted not unlike the mother. "You'd be Nurse O'Donnell's lad – young Healy from Charlestown. Come up and dry yourself." He sounded friendly enough but I was still frightened and unsure. I went up to the fire.

"A bad ould evening – aren't you John-Joe?"

"I am", I said, looking at the heap of clothes and finding myself put off by the smell of the cloth burning. He saw me watching the pile. He lifted a corset from it, held it in his hands waiting for the flames to build up a bit.

"The ould lady went last week – I'm just tidying up."

I was so relieved at his sad news, and to find he wasn't making some sort of a ritual fire, that I almost laughed.

It became a warm and comfortable house when he went and got me a mug of fresh milk and wanted to know if I'd like a warm drop of tea. I told him about the strawberries and he had a bag. When, in an hour, the rain stopped, I went back to the grass where I had left the strawberries, put them in a new bag, picked up the bicycle and cycled home in the dark on a road stiff with new ghosts in every shadow.

Kit could picture it and was amused but, when she got up to go about a job, the old flabby depression settled about her and what she did she seemed to do mechanically.

It was possible now in the daylight to trace in that sagging face the once lovely features: the bone structure was there and, fleetingly – when you managed to knock a smile out of her – the eyes certainly had something of the warmth, life and vitality you associated with this woman.

Theresa was in the wheelchair, idling through a book. We made conversation and it was difficult. Her mother would look at both of us – we were roughtly the one age – and she would turn away and go into the kitchen to do some mechanical thing.

Uncle Pat came home that evening: he had a new light-weight navy suit and a black coat with a velvet trimmed collar.

After dinner he got up and handed the suit to me: "Here, try this on you."

I did as I was told. "That's better. You look less like a greenhorn in that. Now fit this coat on you."

I did.

"That's fine. Now leave the rest here until you are going back to Ireland: while you're here, wear that rig-out and they won't know you are fresh off the boat."

That night there was a Democratic Party function in one of the clubs on the Island and Uncle Pat brought me along with Catherine. Pat was pleased with my knowledge of New York politics. He seemed pleased that his nephew from Ireland was sponsored as a goodwill ambassador by the US State Department in Washington and that I had an accreditation card, signed by the Secretary of State, John Foster Dulles, asking all American officials to extend me maximum courtesy and help. Three times during the night he "flashed" it jok-ingly for some of the local VIPs, explaining that he had, through his nephew, a good connection on Capitol Hill. "Good connections" were, as I discovered, a way of life with Americans.

It was here that I saw Aunt Kit come to something like a bit of life. The group played a few slow waltzes and I took her out to dance. At first she didn't want to dance for she felt awkward, she said. But by the second number she found her feet and was actually enjoying it. I tried an ambitious step which was standard for any old-time ballroom couple and she followed it as easily and as naturally as she must once have danced it thirty years before. I looked at her. Her eyes were smiling richly now.

"You are Stephen's son, aren't you – even to your steps?"

And for a few minutes on that crowded floor the years and the flabbiness seemed to fall from her and she was young again.

When I said to her: "You must have been a good dancer in your day", she laughed back. "What do you mean, in my day: I'm still a good dancer."

I did a quick double-turn and she followed it instinctively. "There", she said, knowing I had tried to surprise her. She was a little flushed as we went back to the table and Pat said it was nice to see Catherine on a floor again.

But already she was Catherine again and the girl who was Kit was gone once more. She fingered her rings and said nothing . . . We returned to the house. Uncle Pat, forgetting, asked me if I'd like to join him in a nightcap. Catherine went to the kitchen. He opened the sideboard, poured himself a drink, put the bottle back and locked the sideboard again, putting the keys in his pocket. Again, Catherine was not asked to have a drink. The pointed locking of the drinks cabinet was now painfully obvious. I began to understand what Aunt Mary meant by her sister having a problem she'd have to the grave.

Catherine said goodnight and went to bed. I asked him about some person we had met at the club who had struck me as a rather forceful character.

Pat smiled. "He's the Schaeffer's man: he got John Flaherty's job when John left them. He will hardly make John's mistake: he's sharp.

"What was John's mistake, Uncle Pat?"

"John was a very big man when he was handing out Schaeffer's free booze at functions like that. Everyone knew him. He was real big

89

when the booze was for free. When they had to pay for it they didn't want to know him . . ."

He finished his drink and the conversation: there was more but he wouldn't say it or tell it.

I was leaving the next morning for Washington but he would be on his way to Brooklyn: he wished me luck and would see me when I finished my tour of duty in Holyoke.

Next morning I put on my American suit, found a billfold in the pocket and a single bill for 100 dollars with his business card. On the back he had written: "Ring if you are in trouble." I said goodbye to Catherine and Theresa and left for Washington to begin my assignment. It would be some time before I pieced together what had happened on Long Island and where Aunt Kit lost the name and the vivaciousness to become the Catherine who seemed to make formal responses to life now, in a luxurious home where she had everything and lived as if she had nothing.

CHAPTER TWELVE

Holyoke, Massachusetts, and its evening paper, *The Holyoke Transcript*, proved altogether an enjoyable and pleasant experience. It is an Irish city, dominated by Kerry families, as far as the ethnic Irish population is concerned.

The Irish had started down on the shanties on the river front and, with every generation after the Famine, the Irish moved further away from the river, up the Hill until now they had made it to the lace-curtain heights, with the Poles and Italians behind them, and the French Canadians ahead of both groups. The latest arrivals on the waterfront in the 'Fifties were the coloured Puerto Ricans.

The Kerry people were so predominant in the Irish community that they could afford to compartmentalise themselves into groupings. Thus you had the Dingle club. You had Dingle undertakers and Kerry undertakers, and because you had a strong Mayo contingent, you had Mayo undertakers, though not a Mayo club. There was as much pride of village among the Dingles as there was among the Cahirciveens and you realised, very quickly, that those immigrants had carried completely their village culture with them to the new world. Indeed the bonding was so strong in Holyoke that it extended and embraced the original home village in Ireland. They were Dingle men in everything but a geographical location. They had their Kerry dances, their Kerry legends, the Kerry meitheal when someone was in trouble, and they made regular pilgrimages to Kerry itself to renew the faith, as it were.

Nearby Springfield was, of course, a great Kerry city: Springfield, Mass., is probably as well known an address in Kerry as any in Dublin.

91

The second strong Irish contingent in Holyoke were "the Connachts": they were the immigrants from Mayo and Galway who seemed to have bonded in the face of the Kerry supremacy. The Mayos were from Belmullet and some from Achill and that in-between point: Inishkea (Inish Gé) Island in Blacksod Bay.

Not all the Mayos had been as successful as the Kerry men who had got there a generation earlier. The Mayos worked in the textile mills or in the paper mills down by the river. Many of them had never been home.

One bright sunny New England spring day I was posting some mail home and passed three men sitting on a park bench watching the squirrels. They recognised me as "the Irishman in the Transcript". I was hailed down.

They told me they were from Achill: they'd been out here "these forty years".

"Did ye never go back?"

"We'll go back when they build the bridge across the Atlantic."

"But sure it's only five hours from Boston to Achill in a plane!", I said.

"The step is a bit long in a plane, young fellow."

"And ye were never home once since ye came out?"

They didn't answer at first. One man said: "We might go the year after next . . ."

I thought of the sunny days in Castleduff and the "vacation" cards from Aunt Kit and Junior: "Hope to see you all next year."

Then another said: "When were you last in Achill? Are the houses still whitewashed?"

There was a tentativeness about the question as if he feared the answer. I told him I had been there a year before I came out. The houses were still neat and whitewashed every spring; they still cut turf with a sleán.[17]

"Now", was all he said. That "now" from an Achill man is a speech. It has a wealth of meaning. It is at once protective, non-committal and bespeaks a doubtful satisfaction or a satisfied doubt.

17. Turf spade.

I learned a lot in Holyoke about America and even more about Ireland and our people. Holyoke had not always been kind to the Irish: it had been a Yankee New England town where the Irish didn't need apply. The misspellings of Irish names in the city directory showed that when they were taken on in the mills on the river front, the foreman who gave them the start very often didn't ask them to spell their names: he spelled them phonetically as they occurred to his German ear or whatever. Pay-cheques carried that spelling and so went into the currency of the city records as corruptions. It was common, for instance, to find one brother in Holyoke spell his name "Cauley" while his brother at home in Mayo was "Cawley".

My stint in Holyoke finished, I had the right to 20,000 miles of "internal travel" within the United States as a guest of the State Department: the itinerary was a matter for myself to decide and to forward to the Washington people.

I did most of the classic tour. I went to Niagara and saw the Falls. I had sung "Moonlight in Vermont" long enough to want to see the actuality. I crossed into Canada and London, Ontario, to see a newspaper friend. I wouldn't miss Detroit and the car industry: walking the Ford Assembly line was to give me a nightmare for years and in it I was chained to that production line. Chicago was another Irish city I collected to see many of my school pals. Denver, Salt Lake City, San Francisco, Los Angeles, Hollywood (disappointed) and on to Albequerque and up the Santa Fé trail to see the Taos Cliff Indian settlement. There were fewer Irish in Houston, Texas, and even less in New Orleans, but New Orleans had jazz still and if the cribs were gone and the pale ghosts of Armstrong hung around the place, there was enough good music still to keep me there for a pilgrim's week.

I saw the "Stars fall in Alabama" and saw segregation as I had seen it in New Orleans. I met an old Irish priest, who had been on the run in Tipperary during the Black and Tan war, and he shocked me by defending segregation: "How would you like a nigger bellying up to your daughter?" was his question when the argument got to its usual deadlocked position.

Carolina looked well in the morning of the late spring/early summer of 1957. I have yet somewhere the name of a Pennsylvania Dutch host who entertained me; the food was luxuriously rich and heavy and eaten out of doors of a June night, with the fireflies darting and pausing and disappearing in the warm trees.

And it was back again to New York and Nostrand Avenue and Aunt Mary. It was easier now. Aunt Mary was glad when I brought in a roast or a few tins of beer for John. John's foot was still giving him trouble: he slept late and seemed to breakfast on the can of beer. The television was switched on as soon as he got up. He went out little enough and took me for one drive: he was going down to City Hall to see about his claim.

I went once more to Long Island. Uncle Pat and Kit had a dinner for me: they invited Pat Junior (of all the letters and cards), and his wife Janet, a lovely and vivacious girl who had produced a child a year and had seven at that time without, as we said at home, them "knocking a feather out of her".

I spent the last day in Long Island, out in the Sound, fishing with young Pat. I stripped to a pair of trunks and with a summer sun beating on us I was sunburned and burned again from the reflected light of the water. I blistered badly.

I suppose we had an Irish wake that night, with Pat and Kit, Junior and Janet and Theresa, with Margie, Pat's daughter by his first marriage, all joining in to wish me bon voyage.

I didn't know then that I would never see Junior again: this sharp cousin of mine who knew the garment district as well as any of the Jewish people who dominated it (and who paid him the compliment of calling him an Irish Jew) would be dead within the decade, of a heart attack.

John Flaherty would be dead much sooner – the lone gosling son who loved them and left them and in the end left Momma to care for herself on the poverty line, helped by Margie who would try and make institutional life easier for her.

I would meet Pat and Kit again but before that I would find out many things about myself and our family and the small holding in Castleduff would come back again into focus in a sharper way . . .

94

CHAPTER THIRTEEN

The Christmas of the year I came back from America, I made the usual trip home to Charlestown to see my mother and collect the Christmas turkey she had on order.

I had all the news of America. I told her how things really were with Mary and Kit.

The Christmas letters had already arrived from Pat O'Neill and Mary. She went over to the press and took down Mary's letter. It had a money order for a hundred dollars. When I told her how Mary had put it together she sat and cried.

"Poor Mary: she always had nature in her . . . poor Mary."

I suppose it was that Christmas, if not the months before, that I began to look at Castleduff and that smallholding and in a slow unconscious way began to see it, and the family it produced, as something of an entity.

Before this it had been the house on the Hill: it was the place where Grandma and Grandda lived. You had the feeling it began with them, was theirs and that they were products of the farm as much as the farm was a product of Grandda's labour.

I had never seen it as the soil from which came Anna whom I never met, Mary, Kit, or Uncle Michael who was to remain a stranger to me. And although my mother went out there regularly during Grandma's and Grandda's days, I never saw it as her home: after all she lived in the town.

Indeed it would take yet another visit to America almost thirteen years later and a remark by my wife in the Algonquin Hotel on her first day in America to sharpen the focus.

We had just spent a hectic day in New York and were back in our rooms when Evelyn said: "You know – people like your mother must have had to grow themselves ten times when they came out here so long ago."

I knew exactly what Evelyn meant. My mother and thousands like her had left a thatched cottage in the heart of rural westland and, never having seen a decent town much less a city, had to come into New York and a bustling, heaving, teeming metropolis and – simply – survive.

For that Christmas of which I write, Evelyn first saw Castleduff. I had decided that whatever the state of relations were between Castleduff and my mother in Charlestown, I was going out to see Jim and Mary Anne and I would find a way of telling Jim how things were with Mary.

Jim, too, that Christmas had got the American letters. Mary had written to him with the usual Christmas cheque and had also written to him early in the summer to tell him of my visit and the talks we had. John, she said, will give you the news.

I didn't give him all the news and what I gave him I gave him gently. Jim was a good man to read me: you didn't have to spell it out.

"She could be better, Jim: she could be better."

The blue eyes clouded: there was no need to say anymore. He blew his nose into a large handkerchief and said: "Now, then." And no more.

He was delighted to meet Evelyn and our youngsters. Mary Anne fussed over them like a clocking hen: she apologised she "had nothing in the house" for them and would they take Christmas cake. Jim had a bottle of whiskey and poured it before I could say I didn't take liquor of any sort – but I'd drink a mug of buttermilk if he had it. He did. There was a small glass of port for Evelyn: it was still the time in rural Ireland when women took nothing stronger than port.

The age lines in Mary Anne's face were marked but her hair was still jet-black. When Evelyn remarked it later to my mother she explained: "Sure she dyes it – she's years older than Jim."

I never knew whether she was or not and it didn't matter to me:

looking back she had, I believe, some form of hormone deficiency which prematurely wrinkles the skin.

But she had made us welcome and I was still "John Joe" or "John agradh" when she addressed me, and she had a great and genuine open wonderment that I had been to America and had seen them all; wasn't I great to do it and wasn't it great to be able to see them?

When we were going, she got in a flap: she had a bit of country butter and I'd take that?

"Now don't go leaving yourself short, Mary Anne."

Sure what is it, agradh, but a small bit – sure I'm ashamed I haven't more. Jim g'up to the garden and cut them a few heads of white cabbage – what kind of spuds have ye in Dublin? Jim, put a lock of them Champions in a bag for them, the seldom they come."

Mary Anne was good-natured: she really couldn't do enough for you and when she had given Jim his marching orders that day, she went out herself and took the head off a fine cock – and apologised he wasn't as big as the one the fox "fuipped" (whipped) three weeks before.

Jim came down to the bottom of the hill to open the gate for the car. We were making our goodbyes when he put his hand in his pocket and took out a coin.

"Here", he said.

I took it.

"It's not a lot", he said, tightening his lips. When Jim tightened his lips like that, things were coming hard on him.

He didn't have to say what he might have said – for his eyes and face said it: "I'd wish it was more." I looked at him and his eyes were filming again.

"Thanks, Jim."

We shook hands. It was not uncle and nephew. It was man to man.

We drove down the boreen to the Charlestown Road. I did not have to open my hand to know that the coin was the old half-a-crown. It was the same generous coin which Grandma had given us all those years ago, when, as kids, we went out to visit her on pension day . . . The road blurred in front of me, remembering.

CHAPTER FOURTEEN

In the years which followed we came and went at summer and Christmas.

I was now of man's estate in my mother's eye: where I went or who I visited was accepted. I was finally entitled to my own judgments and did not have to accept hers and abide by them. If I wanted to go to Castleduff and see Jim and Mary Anne and bring them something, she didn't mind. Now and again – because she never ever let up – she'd tell me that I should be careful because "the strap from Barroe" would think we were going out looking for the holding.

"Sure, look, Mammy – what would I want with the holding. I'm in Dublin and I have all I want: it'd be no use to me." That always seemed to irritate her: it was as if I was somehow insensitive.

I hadn't realised even then that, to her, the smallholding in Castleduff was still the focal point of her life. I suppose that being the oldest son of hers, she expected me to have the same burning ambition as herself to see that the holding stayed in the O'Donnells. I should be as one with her in seeing it didn't go to the "long-tailed crowd in Barroe".

It came up now and again and she'd have the old digs at Mary Anne. Now I could talk a bit better to her and I'd tell her Mary Anne was all right: she does her best.

As the years went on she grew a bit more mellow, it seemed. The first news was that John Flaherty had died. She had been waiting for Mary's death and was surprised that John had gone before her. She was more shocked when the telegram came announcing young Pat O'Neill's sudden death. Junior's death was the last she expected.

The deaths brought Jim and herself a little closer: it was as if they were becoming conscious that death was coming a little nearer all the time. When they met, they didn't have a lot of words to use. They didn't need words to communicate.

My mother would ask about the farm.

What had he in the Bottom Meadow?

And Regan's field?

And the meadow below the Well Field?

Was he cutting in Glosh this year? There was nothing to beat the turf that came from Glosh.

And Mary Anne?

Mary Anne always came last: she was after the cows due to calve, the sow due to farrow, the price for the pigs in the bacon factory in Ballaghadereen and how the calves were shaping.

The answer was always the same: "There's no loss on her."

In actual fact, in those years, Mary Anne worried about Jim.

He was heavy and, although he had a big frame, he had, from his thirties, carried a lot of weight: he had a paunch which no amount of hard work did anything to diminish. He had always been a hearty eater: the more the lump of bacon shivered on the plate with fat, the more Jim walloped into it. Flowery spuds delighted him and Champions were his favourites. A mug or two of buttermilk was no trouble to him before he finished with a mug of strong and well sugared tea.

My mother would tell him he was overweight. He should do something about it. Jim would say it was the nature of the O'Donnells to be stout.

Mary Anne knew Jim was too heavy. When he was in the town, she'd worry until she saw him turn in the mile of a boreen to the house on the hill, cycling slow and steady between the ruts.

"John agradh", she said one day, "I'm mortally afraid he'll be carried into me, dead and ora-wora, what would I do then, agradh, with no one here?

For Mary Anne knew and appreciated more than Jim the growing loneliness of the hill. The immediate neighbours were gone on both sides of the house and now, because of emigration, there were no

99

"scholars"coming down through the farm from the Top Village above on their way to school in Cloonfane.

The scholars, as Mary Anne called them, were the schoolchildren who'd come in twos and threes. They were company in their coming and their going and if they paid a call to the apple trees behind the stablings, well they were only gasúrs.[18] Jim would see them sloping in over the stone fence and he'd wait until they were up a tree, frantically filling small pockets with the red cookers, and then he'd let a roar at them for pure devilment; he'd still stay in hiding to enjoy them going helter-skelter over the fence, their flying legs running up the hill field and home in the Top Village. Jim had little meas[19] on the apples and, as likely as not, he'd hail down one or two of the thieving scholars the next morning to ask them: "Do you want some apples, young fella?"

There'd be a sheepish "yes" and they'd go the road happy.

But now there were no more scholars for the Top Village was thinning out too. You could stand here now and, from the top of the hill, see the only thing which stirred in the fields above and below and to the sides, were the grazing cattle.

The postman came seldom and when you went to Mass on a Sunday, the people you met and talked to had to do you all week until Mass time the following Sunday.

Jim could go down to Davey's for a drink but Mary Anne could not: the singing pubs of the West of Ireland were still a decade or more away and it would be a new day when husbands and wives would then go out for a Saturday night.

But to Mary Anne's generation, the idea of going into a public house was improper and if you offered her whiskey in the house you'd be met with protests: "Ora-wora, John agradh, I could never take that – don't ask me." The point of concession was a drop of port in the bottom of a glass and she'd make prune faces drinking it. ("Sure that's the face she was born with, God help us", my mother would say.)

My mother, of course, was exactly the same about drink and she

18. Young child.
19. Interest.

100

made the same kind of prune faces whenever it was we could coax her to have a glass of punch.

So it was that, when Uncle Pat and Kit came home in the 'Sixties, Kit and my mother determined that they were going to get Mary Anne drunk. They invited Jim and Mary Anne into the house and Pat O'Neill, who had his own liking for a bit of devilment, agreed he'd see to it that Mary Anne would have something more than a drop-drip of port.

"Ora-wora, Pat, that's too much . . . I'd never drink that."

"Here, drink it and stop talking."

She didn't want to offend Pat because he had been "terribly good", meaning he had sent two cheques a year to Jim and herself.

She gulped it.

"Ora-wora, Pat, that was very strong."

"Here – hold your glass: it's only water and sugar."

And he'd top it up again and almost stand over her to see she drank it down.

They made Mary Anne drunk.

But if they did, she got up and danced a hornpipe with a precision which had nothing to do with strong punch and everything to do with the long-forgotten girl in her who had once been a fine step-dancer but who had stopped dancing all those years ago when she first went as a bride to Castleduff.

She was not a young woman then, and maybe it was this and the prim way she held her head – the Feis Ceoil face you see on so many young dancers who take their dancing so seriously – that sent Aunt Kit into a rare fit of laughter which, in the end, brought the tears from her: it infected my mother, too.

It was saved from farce by Pat O'Neill who genuinely marvelled at her dancing and cheered her on. The more he encouraged her, the harder she danced and the sharper she hit the floor with toe and heel, and the more Kit and my mother got hysterical, laughing. I often thought since that Mary Anne knew they were laughing at her and that, at her age, she might seem a ludicrous figure. But she danced for

101

Pat O'Neill that night because Pat had been "terribly good" to Jim and herself.

The dance ended abruptly. She sat down, looking around her as if she didn't know her surroundings.

"Ora-wora, Pat, I'm feeling a bit light in the head."

And with the two sisters sending up a fresh peal of laughter, Pat said: "You're light in the feet, Mary Anne. That was the finest dancing I saw in my life."

Then to Jim, who was "nicely": "You never told me this woman of yours could dance."

It was a compliment and it needed no reply.

They had a good night in Carracastle afterwards but Jim was conscious that it would probably be the last time Kit would ever sit by the fire again: he saw them down the road, him and Mary Anne standing on the hill. Kit was crying, for it was the same road she went almost fifty years before and, if she had more of the world's goods than Jim and Mary Anne, she had less in so many other ways.

When they'd returned to America, my mother was to remember the liveliness of Mary Anne's dancing. It was not funny then for if Mary Anne was that lively she'd survive Jim . . . And, as always, my mother had visions of the long-tailed crowd from Barroe coming into the holding.

Looking back I don't think there was ever a time the Barroes had any designs on Carracastle and the holding. Mary Anne's sister visited her, so did her brother, Charlie, a man with his own holding and an industrious family and he looked after both.

In the end the loneliness of the hill wasn't to be Mary Anne's problem. She took sick and my mother, now well retired as a nurse, went out and did what she could to make her last days easy.

I will always remember the wake-house. Grandma had been laid out on the bed on which she died in the room to the west above the kitchen. Grandda, too, had been laid out on the same bed, the rosary beads twined through his fingers, his moustache, as strong as a mason's, seemed to give his face life and vitality, even in death.

But it was different with Mary Anne. She was coffined and the coffin placed in the kitchen on two chairs. The kitchen was square and big where the other rooms were small. There would be plenty of place for the mourners and the neighbours. She was, they said, a credit to my mother who herself had now fifty years of laying out people, stretching from Brooklyn back to Mayo. Mary Anne may have wasted in her last days but when my mother had finished with cotton wool to push out her cheeks, the neighbours would say that she hadn't looked as well for years.

My mother sat at the head of the coffin and took the sympathies of the neighbours as they came: Jim and myself looked after the menfolk, taking them up to the small sitting room for a drop of whiskey. Or the rest of our family sat the women in relays for tea and ham in the same small parlour. It was four or five at a time.

My mother was at peace now. She could recall Mary Anne's virtues. the hard worker she was. The way she managed for Jim. And there was no one could make butter since M'ma's day but Mary Anne. "And that's the good truth for you, Nora, she was a great hand at the butter . . ."

You would never think my mother regarded her as a "slawmeen[20] Saturday", the woman who was washing all the week and still hadn't finished on Saturday what should have been completed on Monday. There was no sign now of the bad housekeeper who had let all the fine linen sheets she had sent home to M'ma go rotten on the hedges. Who hadn't even the brass candlesticks she had sent home from Brooklyn that the priest might use when Grandda came to pass on. There was no need now to worry about the long-tailed crowd in Barroe. Jim had survived and all would be well in the end.

The long years of slaving in Brooklyn to send home the slates had not been in vain and if the linens were gone itself, never mind . . . The holding was safe now for her and hers. The years of scrimping and saving in Brooklyn had not been wasted.

And so she sat that long night and day, at the head of the coffin, smoothing back an imaginary hair on dead Mary Anne's impassive face.

20. Untidy woman.

My mother wouldn't have understood the word triumphalism but that was the word.

I had no fear for a show of emotionalism on my mother's part when that solemn moment came to close the coffin: she would make the required gestures. The cold forehead would be kissed and it was.

I was right to be afraid for Jim. For all his bigness, for all the strong silence of the man through the wake time, I knew that inside him was the gentler man who could be something of a sentimentalist.

It is very hard to see a big strong man break down and cry like a boy: to put his wet face against the cold wasted breast of this woman for whom we had never once heard him say an endearing word in his life.

I let him cry.

Now, for the first time, my mother cried, looking at Big Jim.

CHAPTER FIFTEEN

I wasn't at home when Jim had his first major heart attack. They took him to Castlebar hospital and he was, predictably, a bad patient. Jim O'Donnell had been a big active man all his life: lying in a hospital bed came hard to him. I went down to visit him when he came home. He could make light of the experience and, being a marvellous mimic, he had stories about the other patients and their troubles. He had taken off some weight and looked the better of it. But he was still very heavy and I knew from the way he was eating that he was ignoring any dietary instructions he had been given.

"Did they give you tablets, Jim?"

"Faith'n they gave me enough to stock Luke Colleran's chemist shop."

"And where are they?"

"They're above on the dresser there."

"Are you taking them?"

"Arrah, what would I be takin' them for – sure I have too much to do."

I tried to explain that as far as I knew, they were to thin down the blood in case of a clot. Jim didn't mind that – he was all right and feeling great, even if he did feel he hadn't as much energy as he used to have.

"'Tis a tightner to walk up the land", he said.

"Of course it is, Jim", I said. "You have to take it a bit easy now you know."

We walked out to the front of the hill as I tried to explain the chemistry of the tablets and what they were designed to do and what you had to do yourself after a big heart-attack.

"Jim, you have to ease up, big and all as you are and strong and all as you feel."

We stopped and he looked at me with those blue eyes of his. He said nothing: the eyes asked the question – was it as serious as that?

"Jim, I'm telling you. You have to ease up. I've seen too many big men like you taken like that." I snapped my fingers.

He looked down the hill, down the road to the Bog Meadow and when I said again he'd have to learn to take it easy, he tightened his lips and said simply:

"There's a wild drop in that field below . . . a man can't turn his back on it."

I knew then how it would be . . .

Jim O'Donnell had worked hard all his life: he knew no other way. There was no other way.

His fields were green. You could stand on the road and look at the hillside and see his fields green where those of his absent neighbours were grey and lean. Slowly I was to realise that his virility in all those long years had been expressed in his fertile fields: they, too might be lean and the ribs of the earth might come through in rocks in fields like the Top Field but they were green where grass grew. His shelter belt of pines was tall and straight.

Thinking back on that afternoon I see him now as the brave bull of the corrida.

He had, with his father, tamed and dominated and made fertile these fields for a century, if you counted Grandda's time. He was strong yet. He would not retreat from the challenge of the wild drop in the field below: he could not turn his back on it.

That night I told my mother what I thought. "Jim", I told her, "will be found dead one morning. It would be either at the bottom of the hill or in the Top Field."

It was very simple. He would not ease up. And since he wouldn't and because the house was in the middle of the holding, whichever way he faced – up or down – he was going to have to put severe pressure on his heart.

"Is he taking the tablets inself?"

106

"No, they're gathering dust above on the dresser. Jim won't take tablets. You know that."

"I know . . ."

And she did. She was as strong and as determined as Jim in her own way.

Sometime before she had to have major surgery. She was over an hour on the operating table in the Bon Secours Hospital in Dublin: she had Dev's team, headed by Dr. Bryon Alton. Alton knew the severity of it. She had, at her age, a fifty-fifty chance of pulling through. That was maximising it, he said: we shouldn't expect too much.

A month later as we left the hospital, Alton took me aside and told me he had marvelled at her will to live: that, as much as anything else, had pulled her through. Had he known my mother better, he'd have known she had to survive to bury Mary Anne and see Castleduff safely back in the family.

On the drive down to Mayo, when I jokingly told her Alton had been worried about her dying, she was back in a flash. "Small fear of me dying yet." She was almost indignant at the idea and you could hear her thinking to herself: "and all I have to do."

Being a nurse, she was a realist. She knew Jim better than most, for, one way or another, they had fought and laughed and mourned together and she knew he had the stubborn and independent O'Donnell streak in him. It was no use talking to our Jim, she'd say.

By now my youngest brother Gerard had married Emmanuel Walsh, a girl, who was - and remains - a mirror image of my mother. The greatest tribute my mother could pay herself and anyone else was to tell us: "I was always a nailer in my day." She was proud that Emmanuel was "a nailer" too. A nailer was someone who was strong, independent, who did the job well, was a good manager and didn't waste any time "playing to the gallery". It was anyone who saved well and spent wisely.

When Gerard brought Emmanuel in, my mother handed over: it wasn't so much a handing over as a genuine sharing, for Emmanuel, she discovered very quickly, was "a girl after my own heart". They

107

were as thick as thieves within the year. Just how thick I discovered one July when I came down from Dublin. They were a long time opening the door and when it was finally opened the two of them came out smiling.

"We thought you were our first tourist", said my mother. Emmanuel saw I was puzzled: "Didn't you hear – we're in the tourist business now, our first paying guest is due this evening." To know why that was such a social milestone in the history of the town, you'd want to understand that my mother always believed in keeping herself to herself.

She had no time ever for the social scene or socialising. Business was transacted in the porch. The friends who were given the right of the kitchen were few: Mrs. Molloy, the bank manager's wife, a few of her Carracastle neighbours, men and women and their families. "Mrs. Healy didn't mix", was how it was put. And now the Healys were in the bed and breakfast business! My mother explained it afterwards to me. For once she was almost apologetic. She thought I might have some misgivings when, in fact, it was the opposite.

"It's a big house and Emmanuel thought the rooms shouldn't go to waste, so she did them up. I let her have at it: they have to pay the rates and isn't she as well having the few pound as the next one?"

"Well, my blessings on her", I said.

"You have to hand it to her – she's a nailer like myself." Most Irish mothers are slow to hand over the hearth to the new woman: my mother might have been no different but for the fact that she recognised, in Emmanuel, a girl as strong and as independent as herself. Now she knew that whatever, her oft-proclaimed prediction (when she was giving out about the Healy side of the family) would not happen: "When I leave, there's not one of ye will keep the slates on the house. The nettles'll be up to the back-door the same as it was when I found yer father in Bellaghy. Skiting around the place – that was all the Healys were ever good for. They'd let the nettles grow up their backsides so long as there was a dance somewhere they could be off to. They left their poor mother without a dinner on Christmas day." (I was a well-grown man before I had the courage to remind her – with a careful jocularity: "You married one of them all the same.")

She never changed: she always had her "sessions". One time she'd be great with one aunt and she'd be out with some of the others. You never knew from one day to the next – or one visit to the next – which of the aunts or uncles were in favour and which were beyond the pale for the moment.

Jim O'Donnell, now that Mary Anne was gone, was "Poor Jim" and he was permanently in favour.

Gerard would go out each day and bring in the cows and milk them. Gerard would have the summer hay and run any messages for him. But try as they might, Jim would not leave the home hearth of Carracastle to go in and sleep "in Nora's".

He'd cycle to Davey's of a night and have a drink or two and cycle back. It wasn't helping his heart condition for the last fifteen yards of the hill were steep. He'd rest as he wheeled the bicycle up. He'd say he didn't know what was wrong with him that he got "winded so easily".

Now "the street", more properly, the yard at the back of the house, began to look a little unkempt. Jim had always kept it tidy. He never carried a forkful of hay to the cow-house that, did he drop a few wisps, he'd pick them up with the hayfork on the way back to the hayshed. There was a place for everything and everything was kept in its place. Now a graip[21] lurched against the dairy: bits of wispy hay were trapped on the bottom bar of the gate. The gate itself was open as often as it was closed and there was a great tiredness about the yard.

The kitchen was tidy enough but you knew there was no woman about the place or a woman's hand on it. The curtains sagged as they were left: my mother would go out every so often and whip them off and take them into town with her to wash them and hang them neatly, they'd stay that way until she came again.

He was the only man on that lonely hill now; the only living thing, within shouting distance in any direction around him, was the dog and the cattle.

21. Fork used on the farm.

109

We got him a television set. The news went through two or three villages by way of the Sunday morning Mass.

One night there came a knock on the front door. As Jim remembered it afterwards, he knew they couldn't be neighbours or they'd not make that mistake. He answered it. The visitors were two elderly men who had been in "the movement" with him fifty years ago. They'd come to tell him that as an old IRA man it was his entitlement to have free television and electricity.

"Arrah, damn and blast them to hell, I told them I didn't want it. Everytime they opened their mouth they titled me and in the end I told them what was done was done. Sure we didn't go out in them days for free television licences." He had the dole and as he used to say it wasn't worth the trouble sometimes. He'd always have to have an eye on the tar road in case the assistance officer came on him in a hurry. Fortunately the road up from the tar road was a good – and slow – Irish mile and that gave a man enough time to hoosh the extra bullock or two over the fence into McGloin's before your man arrived on "the street".

Still and all he got knocked one time on a means test visit and lost "the dole": he took his case to the two Fianna Fáil Ministers in the constituency and they said they could do nothing. It rankled with him, not so much because he lost the few shillings it gave him every week but because, in losing the dole, he had lost a bit of status. After all, as a strong de Valera man and with two Ministers with a shout from the constituency, he expected they'd do something and get it back for him: the dole restored would be his status restored.

In the end he took the case to the Opposition deputy, having spent three months with "his own": in a week he had his dole back and had a long winter to ponder on who had a "shout" above in Dublin and hadn't. I would later inform him that there was no mystery to it, for it was often better to be "well got with the lower orders" than with the top men. My own experience was that that particular opposition deputy, the late and regretted Henry Kenny, was well got indeed with some of the lower orders in Social Welfare!

You can, then, imagine the especial place Charlie Haughey held in

Uncle Jim's eye when, in a Budget decision, he gave all smallholders with farms under £5 valuation the dole entitlement automatically. It was riches for Jim.

He didn't have to watch down the road anymore. Now he could have all the cattle and pigs he liked "and it made no differ" to the means test man.

For Jim it meant he got up of a Monday morning and he had something akin to a week's wages in his pocket. He was sure of that. It was as good as the creamery cheque he used to draw years before: it was "sure money". Jim did what many another smallholder on the snipe grass did: he stocked up with calves. He went to the Agricultural Credit Corporation and borrowed, modestly.

Ten or fifteen years earlier this incentive would have been a godsend to Jim but now time was running out for him. Later in Dublin we would complain about the disastrous increase in our cattle numbers, forgetting that there was a time when we introduced calf subsidies to try and encourage expansion of our cattle population.

I have myself a most vivid memory of the launching of the Second Programme for Economic Expansion by Seán Lemass. A leading agricultural journalist, looking at the projected rise in cattle numbers, facetiously asked Seán Lemass if he really expected every cow in Ireland to drop twins. Lemass, bleakly, answered he was assured the figure was a realistic target.

That we achieved the figures and exceeded them must always, I believe, be attributed to the overnight enterprise of thousands of smallholders like Jim O'Donnell who, relieved of the restraint imposed by the means' test officers' inspections, stocked to the limit.

Anti-dole lobbyists (and some bishops are numbered among them) might care to study the population explosion in cattle which followed the £5 valuation ruling: it disproves the old argument that the dole sapped the smallholders' self-respect and will to work.

Haughey, himself, was to call it, more privately, a subsidy to live on the land. It made an immense difference to smallholders who had survived, like Uncle Jim, and they increased their production by ten or fifteen per cent even though they wouldn't consider their reactions in such economic terms.

With Gerard going in and out I didn't worry too much about Jim. But I was ready for a phone call, some morning or night, to say Jim had gone. I was up and down to Dublin with more frequency now: if I was late, I'd see the light from the main road and know things were all right. I'd carry on into Charlestown and would go out the next day.

Jim had made the farm over to Gerard and it had pleased my mother: now she could run the farm through Gerard and no cow would be due to calve but my mother would know when she was due and wanted, it seemed, a personal account each evening of how each expectant cow looked that day. The arthritis which plagued her might make it more difficult but, when she went out to see Jim, there was little her sharp eye missed as she walked around the yard and house. And she looked after Jim as best he would let her. She tried to coax him to come in and sleep in Charlestown at night, promising him Gerard would run him out each morning in the car.

But Jim was adamant: he would not leave his own fireside.

In the end it was to fall to me to take him from the hearth . . .

CHAPTER SIXTEEN

To this day I don't know why it was that I stopped at the end of the
boreen on my way into Charlestown from Dublin. The normal drill
was to finish the journey at home, have a rest, if not a night's sleep,
and then go out to Uncle Jim's.

There was no reason why this day I should do anything different.
From the main road everything looked normal. There was smoke
from the chimney; the fields looked green. And yet something
prompted me to stop and turn up the boreen to drive over the rutted
road and up the hill to the street. The dog barked at the car. There
was a small porch shielding the back door from the sharp wind from
Mullaghanoe. I noticed a pane of glass was broken. It wasn't like Jim
to allow a pane of glass to go unplaced.

The dog barked but there was no sign of Jim. That wasn't usual.
You'd hardly have made the turn into the road to the house but Jim
would have noticed: he'd be down to open the gate at the foot of the
hill. At worst, as soon as the dog started to bark, Jim would be out
to bellow: "Go back to bed, dog", before positioning himself to
welcome you.

Three young bullocks stared from behind the gate to the Top Field.
He must be up the fields, I thought: he's an awful bloody man. I got
out of the car and opened the back door and went into the kitchen.

He was seated at the table, the top of his body sprawled across the
table top, his head down on the table itself. He lifted his head slowly.
The hat was on the back of his head: his forehead glistened with
sweat. The pain was in his blue eyes.

"You came", he said, grimacing.

113

"What's up, Jim?"

"It's this flaming boot . . . it's too tight on me foot."

I looked under the table. His left foot was stretched out as straight as he could get it. I pulled back the table and knelt down to try and loosen the laces. His foot was swollen grossly. He sat straight back in the chair as I levered off the boot. I watched his face: his lips tightened with the pain of it. I pulled off the heavy woollen stocking but he was still sitting straight back and tensed. The whole foot was swollen.

"Damn and blast that bloody boot but it was tight the first day I got it", he said. But he did not gather the foot up to him: he was still in pain.

"Is that any better, Jim?"

"It's a bit easier."

"How long has it been sore?"

The answer didn't matter and didn't interest me: I had a fair idea of what phlebitis was and I was sure this was it. The swelling was reaching above his ankles and on to the calf of his leg. I flexed the leg slowly and he protested it hurt. For a long time I said nothing: at least it seemed a long time. I know now I was gathering my wits for what was to be one of the toughest ordeals of my life.

I didn't know where to begin or how to begin: I could only stare at that swollen foot and remember all the other days of this big strong man when things were so different . . . the man who paired up with Pádraig Regan to plough a deep straight furrow with Dolly . . . the man who made light work of taking out spit after spit of black turf and had time to laugh between the flying sods. In that silence I could hear the stuck pigs of his lifetime squeal as he plunged the searching knife into the wriggling hearts of them . . . I could feel the disgust and acidity when he forced a five-naggin bottle of porter on my head in the oats field above the house, assuring me it would make a man of me and I only ten . . . above all, the half-a-crown he gave me at the butt of the hill that Christmas when we had met after the neglected years . . .

"Well?"

I lifted my eyes and met his. His face was blurred.

114

"Is it that bad?", he said with a great gentleness.

"You're in trouble, Jim."

He looked straight at me with those blue eyes and he shook his head slowly from side to side. It wasn't bewilderment – just a slow disbelief that it could be anything more than a boot that was too tight for him. For he was still a big man. He still felt strong. He still couldn't see why a big strong man should give in to a tight boot. And yet he knew I wouldn't be upset if I didn't know something was badly wrong.

"You'll have to come in to me mother, Jim: you can't stay here with that foot."

He looked straight at me, even, it seemed, through me. It was as if he wanted to know I would understand what it was he wanted to say next. It was a cruelly long and searching gaze and I knew I could not turn my eyes away.

Then slowly he looked at the fireplace and said:

"There are four fires there . . ."

Slowly the enormity of it dawned on me. His was the last fire in that part of Castleduff and if it was quenched, quenched too were the last hopes of a return of his closest neighbours. It was the old belief and tradition in the power of fire: where there was a fire there was life and the promise of life. So it was when, one by one, his neighbours left for England or America, there would be a "wake" house and Jim or Mary Anne, being the last to leave, would take a blazing sod from the last fire in that house, carry it sputtering and sparking across the fields of the hill to place it on their own hearth as part of the rakings. In that way, although the emigrant's house was closed and the hearth cold, the fire which for so long blazed there, never really went out. There would be continuity, for when the emigrant came home again, he (or she) would take a blazing sod from Jim's fire which had never gone out and, with the tongs which had carried it, bring the new blazing sod back to the old hearth to relight a new fire.

I looked at the fire. There was a clatter of tongs there and between heads and tails I counted four.

"You understand now", he said, very simply. It wasn't stubbornness had stopped him from going into Nora's to sleep of nights. It wasn't the traditional attachment a man has for his own fire and his own hearth. His was the last fire and it had three fires in it, kept in trust for families who would one day come back. If this fire went out it was the last living thing which bound the neighbours to return, for he knew the word would go that Jim O'Donnell's fire, the last fire on the hill, was quenched . . .

I stood up. He sat there, his left foot still straight out in front of him, looking at me with those questioning clear blue eyes, waiting, one boot on, one foot bare in that sparsely furnished kitchen . . .

I could think of nothing but the brave bulls of the corrida who, worked almost to the point of exhaustion, have ceased to charge, and now, with their backs to the barrero, stand and wait, eyes on the matador, who is himself facing up to the moment of truth when he goes in over the horns.

"I must stay", he said, "I'll over it – I overed worse in my day."

"Jim: its up to yourself. How do you want to go down to Carracastle? In bits and pieces? How do you want to die? A bit at a time? That foot there. Another two days and you'll have to leave with the pain of it. They'll take you to Castlebar and they'll take it off from the ankle. After that, it'll be from the knee. Then the other foot. And the other leg, from the knee . . . That's how it is, Jim. Now which way do you want to go to Carracastle . . . how do you want to die?"

And because my eyes were as choked as my voice, I ran from that kitchen and stood at the door and cried until I could cry no more.

After a long time I heard Jim blowing his nose. I went back in.

"I'll go as far as Nora's."

"All right, Jim."

I raked the four fires, fed the dog and, with a slipper over his bare left foot, helped him into the car. I put the hasp on the door and we drove down the hill and the rutted road to the tar road and into Charlestown. I went in first to alert my mother and she came out to help him out of the car.

"She said: "Jim agradh, it has come to this?"

"It has come to this, Nora."

She seated him on a high chair and she looked at his foot.

She didn't have to look at it twice.

"It has to be Castlebar, Jim agradh."

"Well, let it be Castlebar then."

The break had been made with the hearth and the fires. He could be stoical now. Gerard made arrangements with the local doctor to have him admitted and then the two of us drove him to the hospital.

They gave us a wheel-chair to take him in. Two cheerful nurses joked with him. One of them recognised him from his previous stay: she remembered his good spirits. Inside another sister recognised me: "Is this man a relation of yours?"

"This man is much closer than the uncle he is to me – look after him well for he is one of a great people." He was pleased. Twenty minutes later when we saw him again, he was on a couch, cracking jokes with the doctor and nurses.

He had a great heart. A big heart. In the end it took a series of massive seizures in Castlebar to make an end to Jim O'Donnell.

We brought him to Carracastle and the hearse stopped at the boreen. His fields were green. His cattle were well-fleshed. The plantation was standing tall against the proud gable of the house on the hill.

There was Kevin, Gerard, Aidan (June's husband) and myself to carry his coffin. I saw Pádraig Regan, his team mate of all the ploughing years, and knew that he wanted under the coffin. I nodded to him and together we put him on our shoulders and laid him to rest beside Mary Anne.

Silent Pádraig wept too . . .

CHAPTER SEVENTEEN

We went back to Castleduff after the funeral. Stiff knee or not, my mother was all business.

"Gerard, you'll get a pane of glass for that window."

"That hedge can do with cutting back. The cow-house hasn't been cleared for two days – you'll do that now before we go in. Did the hens lay? There must be some eggs in the hay."

Inside she had the lace curtains off. "I'll bring them in and wash them", she said.

She found some old linen in the bottom of a press, mildewed.

"The Lord of mercy on the dead. Poor Kit."

She'd bring that in and wash it and iron it, too. "Poor Mary Anne – sure God help her, she was never used to linen, the poor thing."

She was making an inventory and it was easily made. Now and again she'd come across what remained of something she had sent M'ma from Brooklyn forty years before. "Poor M'ma – she loved anything fine. She had more pillow cases with a bit of embroidery on them . . ."

She came across a pair of brass candlesticks she had sent home in a Brooklyn parcel. They had been packed away years ago. "An' I thought they were gone."

We were looking at the small flotsam and jetsam which remained after two generations of the O'Donnells. She rooted out something else which had come from Pat O'Neill's store. "You'll have that", she said. "Jim would like you to have that."

I demurred.

In strict point of fact it wasn't in my mother's giving: what was here was now Gerard's. I have always had a slight squeamishness about moments like these. Even at an auction in a private house I feel there is something not right about seeing the personal effects and bric-a-brac of someone's life up for sale: of seeing what must have been very personal things, with memories, pawed and turned over and fingered and then rejected. Later Gerard would insist I had something from Castleduff and I told him about Grandma's clock. Being as full of good-nature as he is, he insisted on my taking it.

I took one other thing: a knobbled ash-plant which Grandda had cut and shaped with use. He had driven cattle with it and Jim after him. Jim had cut his own and now the two of them lay inside the back door.

I walked out to the hay-shed. Half the covered area was used for storing turf. Here, gathering quiet rust, was the social history of this smallholding. Grandda's reaping hook. It used to gleam after he cut rushes for thatching and haystacks in the gairdín . . . three scythes and two sharpening stones . . . an old loy, one corner broken but still sound . . . old cutting blades from the mowing machine, the last of which was rust-eroded under the pines. It was awful easy then to read the history of our people in that few square yards of bric-a-brac and to trace how a changing technology, the great word of our day, had played its role in changing the culture patterns of smallholdings like this.

Above in Dublin now we were already worrying about the cultural impact of electronic technology and the effect which television, with its Anglo-American values, was having on rural Ireland. We talked about it as if it was the first wave of technology and the only one which would have a fearsome cultural spin-off.

On the side of this part of the hill it was an academic argument: many of the houses were empty and all the waves of ad-massery could sweep over this hillside and it didn't matter. Another, and earlier, technology had already altered the cultural patterns and we had never recognised it or what it was doing to our people.

The rusted reaping hook was the last of the old technology: it had been the basic implement for centuries. It was slow work but it

119

predicated sharing. It produced the meitheal and all that sprang from the meitheal.

The scythe replaced it. The scythe halved the meitheal in numbers as it cut meadows and oatfields in half the time. And then before we had even adjusted to the change, the horse-drawn mowing machine slashed the necessity for the meitheal and the men of the meitheal even further. Pádraig Regan and his horse would team with Jim O'Donnell and his horse and mowing machine and they'd do in half a day what a meitheal of scythes would take two days to take out.

If a third was needed at all, it was a woman or a boy, who'd follow the mowing machine to fork out the heavier swarths when they piled up on the cutting blade. We didn't miss the young men in their going or the young women who went after them: we thought when the first tractor came in to the village and bulled its way into the small meadows and did in an hour what it took two men and a pair of horses half a day to do, it was a great and efficient machine.

The bull tractors wanted only one man and you didn't have to feed him or drink him: you just gave him his money and he moved on over the village to the next job.

The tractor cut wide swathes in our already fast-dwindling population. It cut out Pádraig Regan and his horse pairing up with Jim O'Donnell and his horse for the spring ploughing and the summer hay-cutting. It cut out the meitheal of carts drawing turf from the bog and hay into ricks or hay-sheds. The first spring meitheal of turf-men would follow when, much later, the Sugar Company turf-cutting machine arrived. In the autumn the ubiquitous tractor, with yet another multi-fitting, would reduce the need for the few who remained.

The sickle or the reaping hook had evolved over the centuries as a piece of technology. Here, on this farm, it had been used by Grandda, in preference to the new-fangled scythe which he accepted with reluctance. In forty years of rapid technological change, the Jim O'Donnells learned how to master the new technology but never realised, no more than did our political leaders, that every new technology exacts a price in the social as well as the economic organisation of our people.

120

Jim O'Donnell never got a tractor. He would not give in to the rush to mechanise: he stayed with the mowing machine and the plough for his own use. He had two good machines in his hands and the sleán was only an extension of those machines when it came time to go to Glosh.

It was all there now . . . from the loy to the rusting coulter of the Pierce plough which broke the rock-ribbed land and burst the bog-sod: the sickle to the rusting mowing machine, or what was left of it, which had gathered in the fruits of the loy or the plough.

The other and bitter fruits of this technological revolution were on this hillside now.

Directly over the remains of the mowing machine, across the Well-Field, Towey's house stood silent. Behind me McGloins was empty. The land was out on conacre. The bullocks had replaced people and now even the bull tractors were fewer and some were already rusting, too, because everyone wanted to be independent and have the new status symbol. When bullocks come in, men and machines go out.

We may cry about losing our language: we lost as much again when we lost the meitheal. Yet in Dublin today we are experiencing newer and more powerful technologies and we are, in our economist-dominated society, admiring their potential and measuring their poss-ible applications in economic terms only. We have not yet learned to appraise them for the social consequences they may have for what's left of our rural society, to see how we can be masters of the technology rather than slaves dragged unthinkingly behind it.

The time span from the reaping hook to the tractor is half a century. The technology is a low-grade one. But consider what it did to the social pattern of life in the Castleduffs of rural Ireland. Yet we hailed each stage as "labour-saving" and a boost to "increased produc-tion". We could measure time and sweat saved in a hayfield; we failed to invent a machine capable of monitoring the fearful social cost of the new technology so that, by better direction, we might have obviated some of those damages by a planned redistribution of what resources we had, and still have . . .

121

The loy I took later and gave to a folk-museum in Bonniconlon where artefacts of a disappearing age were being treasured. Later still Gerard gave me the spud-pot in which Grandma used to boil the Aran Banners for the pigs and the skillet pot for baking bread: they are in Achill today.

Just as I did the morning after I had left Jim in hospital, I cleaned out the cowhouse. There is a rich warm brown smell to cow-dung which I can inhale with an almost sensual satisfaction. There is only one smell better. It is when the drain is swept clean with a yardbrush and things are tidy, you fill your arms with crisp hay and place it at the head of the stalls. Step back then, when the job is finished, and the aroma is one of hay and cows and the lime of the whitewash and the smell of warm milk. Twenty-five years of printers' ink and hot metal and the fug of a newsroom cannot drown that out anymore than it can ever give you the rich satisfaction you got when Jim's plough opened up the dark sod on Charles O'Donnell's conacre field, the first ploughing it had for forty years because Mr. de Valera's tillage inspector was down "expecting the land" as a local Mister Malaprop had it.

I went back into the kitchen. My mother was busy tidying up. The broken window she explained. Apparently the day I happened on Jim, he had tried to open the back door to go out and blow the whistle in the hope someone would hear it. The door jammed. All he could do was take the ash-plant and break out the pane of glass. He blew and blew but, of course, there was no one on the hillside to hear him . . .

All the money he had was in his pocket and I still remember that after all the years of working and slaving to make ends meet, it shocked me to think that I had often left more in a Dublin restaurant for a night's outing.

Later Gerard would find out he owed the Agricultural Credit Corporation a few pounds and we wondered where it had gone. It wasn't a great deal but Gerard knew he had not used it to add stock in the loan period. It would be much later still, as Gerard went about the task of putting things in order, that he'd find naggin or half-naggin bottles, empty, hidden away in the stone fence here and there. He had his own way to numb the desolate loneliness of the years without

Mary Anne or to blunt the angry frustrations he felt when he was silently forced to recognise he was not the big strong man he once was, able to dominate his fields in the old way, having to leave more and more to this gentle young nephew of his who was not born of the land but who was doing his best, and was, as he was to tell me, "shaping up well".

I put on the television to hear the news from Radio Éireann. My mother was ready for home. It had the usual quota of items. One was a report to say that when we joined the EEC, under the Mansholt Plan, there would be little or no future for the traditional smallholdings. By now it was what I called the familiar jazz-bit: we had heard it before many times in Dublin.

"Turn that damn thing off. Have you no respect for the dead?"

It was my mother. At first I thought it was the usual thing we had always observed when someone died. You didn't switch on the radio, or generally, do anything because there was supposed to be a period of mourning where even the clocks were stopped in a solemn silence.

But the more I think of it since – because she didn't object to the television being switched on – I wondered if the annoyance didn't spring from the news item itself.

And who would blame her if, after all the years and all her working and planning and scheming and fighting to see the holding back in her family, she would resent anyone, Eurocrat or whatever, telling her that it was all one great waste of time?

Outside she took a look at the cow-house I had cleaned, noted the fresh hay and said: "That's good . . . that's good."

Satisfied, she eased her stiff leg into the car and, very contented, we drove down the hill, down the boreen and on to the tar road.

She looked back from the road at the silent house.

"It's a fine, tidy holding."

She was immensely pleased . . .

CHAPTER EIGHTEEN

It was perhaps the next summer that Uncle Pat O'Neill, a widower for the second time, came home to Ireland again. He crossed this time in an Aer Lingus Boeing and, since I had the flight number, I rang some friends in the company and, explaining who he was, asked them if they'd arrange to have a bottle of his favourite whiskey, Chivas Regal, laid on for him. Aer Lingus do things more than very well and Uncle Pat got the VIP treatment on the flight and was "nicely" when he was decanted by the hostess with great gentleness at Dublin Airport. I thanked her for looking after him. I think it was the other way around, she said, smiling. Pat in his seventies still had the goaty eye. God bless him! My mother, fur-coated, met him again and there was still a thing there after all the years.

That night we had the "do" and the old days were relived by the two of them and, after crying the dead, they were happy again. The laugh is as close as the tear with the old people.

Pat went home to Charlestown with Gerard and my mother. Later he went to his own home in Donegal, staying at a local hotel. I joined him there to drive him around, taking a few days off. His brother's daughter was married to a salmon fisherman/small cottier at Inver and she made him very welcome. The home was snug and clean and Pat liked that: he was proud of her and her home. He asked me to drive him to the beach on which he used run bare-footed as a youngster.

It was a warm sunny day and the sand was hot. He stopped and looked at it. Nothing had changed in the fifty years. Time stood still here. He sat down, took off his shoes and stockings and we walked without talking. The powdered sand oozing between his toes and the smell of sea-wrack peeled away the years. He stopped once, and behind his glasses his eyes were misted, remembering.

The laugh which came was a nervous one: he remembered some boyhood incident – a chase the length of the beach – and he was all right again. We went to the water's edge and he paddled through the ebbing tide waters. For that hour New York and its triumphs and its tragedies were far away . . . his first wife . . . Pat Junior . . . Kit and Mary Flaherty and her gosling son, John.

At the end of the visit, Kevin and I took him to the Martello Tower in what is now the New Jurys. It was then one of the better late-night dinner spots in Dublin. Pat liked it. More accurately he was very pleased that Nora's sons knew how "to do things in style".

We talked over the holiday. He had enjoyed it greatly. He was saddened, however, with one thing: after all he had sent home, he thought his old home-place should have looked better. It didn't take much to keep the blackberry briars cut back. But his Inver niece and her tidy home pleased him. All his money wasn't a waste. And Nora made good use of the little he sent: it was nice to be with her sons and see they had done well for themselves. Above all he liked to see they had "a bit of clout" in the capital city or at least enough to get him VIP treatment with the national airline.

All of it had nothing to do with some creature comforts on a transatlantic plane or what hospitality might have been extended: it had everything to do with seeing and appreciating what he regarded as a rich dividend on the investment he had made over his lifetime in "sending home".

Afterwards he would write to my mother and tell her how proud he was of the way the family had turned out: if only some of the others on whom much more had been spent had made half the use of the help, he'd have been a happier man.

Poor John Flaherty was a bit of a disappointment to him, my mother said. It wasn't the amount of money involved: it was just that he didn't handle it right. Pat was a businessman and, for all his wealth – and it was substantial – he always looked after the dollar. When he spent, he spent wisely: when he invested, he expected to see the percentage come up. It was as simple as that. You made an investment and when the percentages came up right, you said so. If the investment went wrong, you said little. He said little enough to my mother about John's tavern going wallop; merely that he tried to give him a hand: it amounted to about 20,000 dollars. He excused the failure with no more than "John hadn't a head for business" and left it there.

We left him to the plane. He would come again: it was so much faster than coming by ship. Maybe next year – or certainly the year after next.

He didn't come the next year but he "sent home" to my mother and told her he'd be visiting us the year after. He was down in his holiday home in Florida where he'd spend the winter months.

He didn't come that summer and he went down to Florida in November. The robin outside the backdoor at home was in full throat and my mother knew there'd be a letter from Pat for Christmas. So there was. The robin sang through Christmas Eve and Christmas Day.

On St. Stephen's Day the robin did not sing and the news came that Pat O'Neill had been found dead in his apartment. He was alone and apparently had been dead for thirty-six hours before his neighbours realised it. They brought him back to New York to bury him beside Kit and Pat Junior: his oldest son by his first wife, Fr. Joe O'Neill, a Maryknoll missionary priest down in Terra de Fuego, flew back for the burial ceremony. It was a big funeral: he was a big man.

Today he makes generous dust, his last tithing to the country which took him in, a raw boy from Donegal, with nothing more than a willing pair of hands and a good head. In fifteen years he would not merely walk the setts he had first laid in Brooklyn but would come to have his first piece of property in the borough and, from it, and his business, there flowed the thousands of dollars which he sent home to Donegal and Carracastle and Charlestown, to his own and to Kit's people. His generous seeding stretched from Donegal in dollars to Terra de Fuego in his priest son and through the rest of his children of that first marriage, for they looked after Aunt Mary and made her last days less lonely on the poverty line of New York.

Later still they would help his last daughter of the second marriage in her slow decline. Theresa, mercifully, did not survive half a decade after him but needed constant nursing which she got in generous measure from her older stepsister Margie and Fr. Joe, who would spend his vacation taking her out and about or merely sitting with her attending to her physical needs hour after weary hour of a long day.

Fr. Joe wrote later with the news in detail for my mother. She read it and reread it and read it again.

"They're all gone now with Pat, and I'm thinking I won't be long after them", she said.

Her stiff knee seemed to be stiffer now and, although I joked and said she'd see more of them down before she was ready to go herself, I realised that for the first time a little bit of the zest to fight against the stiff knee – which was really a fight against the advancing years – was going out of her.

A bit of her died with Pat O'Neill: more than had died with her three sisters, Anna, Mary and Kit.

She was not a sentimental woman: she had seen death too many times in her life. She had seen it in New York in The Plague of the Spanish Lady: the great flu epidemic which reached in and took her sister. She knew how to set her face against death: you worked and you did not sit around moping, as she'd say. Life had to go on and life went on at an increased pace so you didn't have time to think about it. She despised the weakness of self-pity.

When my father died, she did what had to be done and then she went back to the work, busier than ever. She had little time for the conventional sympathies of her neighbours in the district and, while she wouldn't snub them, she always made sure to busy herself even as they fumbled with the consoling words which, inevitably, included "sure I remember when my own man went on me". Or some such experience.

There was no self-pity in my mother's book and she'd come in from such a "call" and explode in the privacy of the kitchen: "These people sicken my backside", and she'd pick up the twig and sweep the floor vigorously as if to purge it.

127

She could not tolerate pity or self-pity: they were blemishes. And so it was even when her oldest daughter, my sister Marie, died in England in her first confinement.

Marie had gone to England to train as a nurse. She was the image of my mother in temperament. We used to call her "witcheen" because she had a temper if you "rose" her: when you did, you were better to get out of her way. She was third in our family but if you said "witcheen" or "cocked noseen" (she had a pert nose) it was only prudent to have scouted the ground for a quick exit first.

For two generations my mother had delivered the women on the district: she had, they said, "lucky hands". She never lost a child.

Nowadays most of the women opt for the county hospital and, indeed, in the last year or two before her retirement, the vogue of going into hospital to have your baby was already starting. Most of the young mothers then were women she had delivered herself in farmhouses or wherever. Where their mothers were still alive, they'd tell the daughters: "You should have Mrs. Healy: she has lucky hands."

Many of them did. Her "lucky hands" were no more than a passionate commitment to good hygiene. When the expectant mothers came to her in the closing months of the confinement, she'd drill into them, mercilessly, the need for hygiene: the things they needed to do and what to leave ready for her and have in readiness for the baby. She delivered two generations of the Wards. They were tinkers and she loved them. They would range as far as Enniskillen but when Rose or Biddy or Ann Ward's time was near, they packed their gear and traps, their bits of tin and sticks of solder and made for Charlestown and "Nurse Hail-ey". (Not Healy, Hail-ey – the old "E" fada.)

Today we call them itinerants and we've organised to help them off the side of the road and the primitive conditions under which they lived. The last of the Wards are still on the road, men and women delivered by my mother in cold, wet camps made of sugar-bag sackings stretched on sally rods which backboned them like thin ribs.

But Rose or Biddy or Old Anne were never confined but they too had their menfolk – whatever the night and however wild it might be –

128

boil the water she'd need before, during, and after the delivery. They'd have a sparkling clean sheet and, even if the dust and ashes from the fire blew into the wobbly tent itself, she'd have a sheet which she'd brought with her to curtain off the woman in labour so that the children would not see, even if they heard, the shrieks of the labour pains.

The curtain wouldn't keep out the smoke of ash and hawthorn or whin cipeens but it kept out most of the dust and the prying eyes. The carbolic soap was always part of her maternity bag kit, and she used it liberally. There'd be a rally of the tinkers for a birth as much as for a funeral. And when the confinement was over and the new child "christened" with a drink-up, old factional spleens were, as likely as not, to start in the encampment. There'd be a rush for "Nurse Hailey" as a peacemaker and I remember one night, around one in the morning, she was called out with shouts of "They're murderin' her: they're murderin' her", and she climbed up on the fixed wheel bicycle in the pelting rain and off down the Ballymote Road, fearing for the life of the young mother whom she had delivered twenty-four hours before. She quite expected to find the recuperating mother beaten black and blue by some of the women: when she arrived, there was a dead silence. This particular girl had a horse-drawn caravan and my mother climbed the steps with the father expecting to find a young mother "stretched". Instead they found her sitting on the bed, wary and alert and the handle of a pick-axe in her hand still.

"Are they gone yet?", she asked, explaining some of the women had come and tried to topple over the caravan with her and the child in it, and when that was too much for them, one had gone to get lamp oil "to burn the bitch and her brat".

She didn't wait – she got up out of her weak bed, grabbed the nearest thing to her and jumped from the steps to lay all about her, left, right and centre until they panicked and ran with sore heads and blue arms and backs.

They were hardy, tough women but my mother followed them to their camp and warned them that if they laid a hand on the girl and her child, they'd come to a bad end – and damn the one of them, seed

129

or breed, would she attend again as long as she was "on the district". That cooled them a bit and maybe the drink had worn off but, as one of the older women assured her: "Sure we have to be said by you – where would we be but for your lucky hands, Nurse Hail-ey."

It was to be the grim irony of her professional life as a nurse, and her private life as a mother, that her own qualified daughter, with the most medically up-to-date gynaecological services around her and the best of skilled doctors and specialists with whom Marie had worked, should, in the end, be able to do nothing for her to save her life or that of her baby. Her husband, Ken, a lovely lad, rang us with the news that trouble had developed. He described it accurately and well and said the doctors were hopeful.

My mother was not hopeful: when she heard the details, she knew. "Marie is finished." Four days later Marie was dead. She must come home to be buried in Carracastle. She was. We stopped the funeral at the bottom of the boreen leading to Uncle Jim's and paused for the minute. A lark sprang up from the heather, loud and clear, in a shaft of sudden sunlight. We went the short distance to the graveyard. Jim and Mary Anne were there . . . Pádraig Regan and all the women she delivered for close on four decades. Most of them sensed the awful irony of it: her own daughter to die in childbirth.

She cried her fill at the grave but as she came away, she was already master of herself: life would go on – there would be things to do and she would do them. That strap Mary Anne was still on the hill of Castleduff and Jim could go anytime and then the holding would be sure to go to the long-tailed Barroes. Did ye see them at the funeral? It wasn't up to bury the dead they came but looking to see how our Jim was: they were always the hungry crowd down there.

It wasn't so, of course, for there was nature in the MacManuses too and, if Nora O'Donnell was in trouble, where else would they be but in the graveyard for she and hers stood with them in their bad hours. I knew then she would never rest until the holding was safe for some of her own: she had to live to see that done.

The arthritis was already in on her but she would come up to Bryan Alton for the deep injections which gave her some easement. They were always painful for her but she tightened the small mouth against the pain. It would be as nothing to the pain she would live with all her life if the Barroes came to Castleduff.

And so she put aside self-pity, bossed us all when we came within her reach, drove us on, cautioned us here, and encouraged us there. She did not relent, not ever.

The arthritis grew worse but she would not use two sticks and they'd never see her hobbling like poor Girlie Walsh who was crippled with the same complaint and shuffled her way along on two walking sticks.

It took generous Pat O'Neill's death and the realisation that he was the last of them in America, to face her with the passing years.

She, in her turn, wouldn't be long after them.

CHAPTER NINETEEN

You got used to the routine.

Gerard would call on the phone: "Look, when are you coming down again?"

"Anything wrong?"

"No – just Mammy was wondering when you'd be down like: she's due for a check with Alton."

"How is she?"

"All right, you know. Just that she'd like to know when you'll be coming down: she has to arrange it with Alton."

"I'll go down the weekend."

She always looked well even if her knee was stiff.

Emmanuel and Gerard had produced their first son, Stephen. The cattle were going well for Gerard. Emmanuel had decorated the house, room by room: she had replaced the original windows which were draughty with big teak plate-glass windows. The water was finally installed and she had the comfort of a bathroom and indoor toilet now. Gerard was on the post and had a car so that "he wouldn't kill himself cycling like his father before him, out in all sorts of weather."

She was all right but the knee was "killing her". That meant that she couldn't move around with the brisk efficiency she always had. "Suff go deo on the knee", she'd say as she'd heave herself out of the chair slowly. The knee, you would understand, was somehow outside the rest of her.

"You want to go up and see your boy-friend, Bryan Alton?"

"It'll do me no harm to have a check."

"A wonder you wouldn't go up on the train now that you have free travel."

"Throt'n I won't: I'm not that badly off yet that I want free travel, with two of ye above in Dublin with cars under ye."

I had been joking of course, I knew her too well to ever see her producing her old-age pension book. It was no use saying to her that she had paid her taxes all her life and we were paying them now so that she could have that amenity. To her the free travel was like the free beef long ago: she'd starve herself and the family before she'd ask for a hand-out.

I brought her up and she stayed with Kevin and myself for a few days before and after the check in the "Bons". She was in good form and lively enough but she was stiffening up with the knee. Lately her stomach had been "against me", as she'd put it: maybe it was the old ulcer back again. Once we got on the road for Charlestown she seemed contented. It was a warm July day, the kind I like when driving home. We came to Ballaghadereen where my sister Junie is married. We stopped: she wouldn't go in. Junie came out to welcome her home and they chatted and talked for half an hour in the car: June would go over that night to see her at home.

Now when she had to sit for two or three hours in a car, she always found herself stiff. There's a short drive from the road up to our house at home: the incline isn't much but I felt that, after a run like that, it would be better to open the gates and drive her up to the back gate at the side: all she'd have to do then was lift the foot over the threshold of the low wicket gate and another step up onto the concrete apron at the back of the house and walk in. The distance is, at best, fifteen yards.

Between the effort to get her out of the car, with Gerard and Emmanuel helping me, it took her almost half an hour to cover that short distance. She blamed the long sitting on the way down from Dublin: she'd be all right when she got into her own room and bed again. She had a cup of tea and a piece of toast and then Emmanuel helped her into bed. She fell asleep. I returned to Dublin.

Gerard rang me each night. He wasn't happy with how things were.

133

My mother wasn't eating: she showed no interest in eating. He had Dr. O'Brien up to see her. He wasn't happy with her condition either.

Was she up and walking around? No. The night she came home she had tried getting out of bed to go to the toilet and Emmanuel had found her on the floor. She was a bit too heavy for Emmanuel on her own. Emmanuel had told her if she wanted to get out of bed, just to call her and she'd help her. Later again that night Emmanuel found her again on the floor. She did not call.

I tried to contact Bryan Alton: he was out of town. It didn't matter for I knew how things would go now. Gerard brought her to Castlebar Hospital and there we were with her. She looked great and she looked strong. They were feeding her intravenously with a glucose drip. She didn't want it and I very soon realised she had made up her mind to die.

She was a professional to the end: she would not ring and did not ring once for a doctor or a nurse. Her bedside bell was never used unless it was by some of us when we thought a nurse might be able to make her more comfortable.

It took her two weeks to die. By this time her arm was almost blue-black from the drip. Evelyn and I were in Achill and could get up each night: Junie and Gerard came over from Ballaghadereen and Kevin and Una came all the way from Dublin twice a week or more. Faithful Fr. Peter – then a Canon of the diocese — came up from Ballymote with Aunt Agnes Healy and it grieved them to see her steadfastly seeking death.

In a half coma from drugs, you could see her mouth tighten with the pain but never a sound passed her lips. There were no complaints. No self-pity. For this too, was like any other task she had set herself: it would be done with all the ability and strength she had.

One afternoon we came up from Achill. We sat for an hour, watching her in that half-sleep, silently registering the pain in the tightened lips. A few of her old patients came over from Charlestown: they knew her well enough to know that she'd resent their seeing her lie there helpless, this woman who was once a tower of strength and courage. But they came and risked her annoyance, for she had stood by them in their hours of labour and distress.

134

Now she was past annoyance. They stood there and wept to see her great frame almost stilled: the pain on her lips as she fought her own last battle to die, alone and private.

Her well-fingered rosary beads she did not want: her prayer book, stuffed with the memoriam cards of half a lifetime, until, it seemed, there were more cards than pages between the shiny black covers, was now untouched. She had passed beyond the world of prayers and the rosary and the novenas: all that remained was to cross the threshold of pain to release.

Once, she regained full consciousness that afternoon. Now the pain was in her blue eyes.

"It's you . . .", she said.

"Yes: don't talk too much now. You must try and eat . . . you know that. Your old boy-friend, Alton, says you are in great shape: you know what he said about your heart – it has the strong beat of a woman half your age." So it had.

She looked at me through the pain in those blue eyes and it was hard to watch without flinching.

"John agradh, I have gone the road as far as I can and I have done what needed to be done. You'll see to Kevin and Gerardeen – they're good lads, Junie will be all right – she has a good man."

I wet her lips: she fell asleep. I was not to hear her speak again. Four slow long days later she was dead.

She had never once called a doctor or summoned a nurse. She never once complained. She had lived like a professional and she had, once she made her mind up, died with as much dignity as death allows to any of us.

There wasn't a wrinkle on her fair skin in the coffin: she looked young, far younger than Grandma at her age. Only the lower lip betrayed any signs of that last struggle: it seemed set still as if, in death, she still feared a cry of self-pity might pass them.

We brought her the road to Carracastle: the old familiar road of her working life, past Lavey, past Gowel, past the school of Cloonfane where she had got the bit of national schooling she was to make do with for a lifetime in two countries.

At the end of the boreen to Uncle Jim's we stopped again. The fields were green and fresh: the bottom meadow was cocked and ready for taking in. The cattle were in fine condition and there would be good aftergrass. The patch of oats was ripening. Castleduff was safely in her son's hands.

It was fifty years ago or more on this spot she had left M'ma for America, a young green girl from under the thatch who went with the one and old farewell: "Keep your mouth and your legs closed: keep your ears open – and send home the ticket for Kit."

Well she had done that. She had done more: she came home with the slates to take her parents out from under the thatch and the summer sun now shone on those same red tiles on the house on the hill. She had helped to keep the heart in the land with her cheques from America and those of Kit and Anna and Mary, and Pat O'Neill.

She had fought with Jim and she had fought with Mary Anne: she had fought with the long-tailed crowd from Barroe and she had won.

Along part of that hill some of the houses might be deserted and the fields peopled with bullocks but O'Donnells still had a fire in it and the grass, thin as it might be, with the rocks coming through the ribs, still was in the family.

It was no easy road but she travelled it well. I knew when the hearse moved on for the short remainder of that road to the graveyard in Carracastle where she would lie with her husband and her dead daughter, Grandma and Grandda, Jim and Mary Anne, she would rest easy now . . .

EPILOGUE

This has not been an easy book to write: it may not be an easy book for my family to live with at first but in the end I hope they will come to appreciate what it is I have tried to do and say; not only about my mother's family, but for all the families like hers whose struggle, just to exist, is part of the story of modern Ireland.

Today there is a concerted international campaign which seeks to dismiss the smallholders, not merely of Ireland but of Western Europe, as barriers to economic progress. Their holdings are regarded as rural slums and Euro-bulldozers wait impatiently in the wings to plough them under in the mistaken doctrine that big is beautiful. It may be so.

We may not be able to stop them – but at least I, and my neighbours, will have this small satisfaction: the Eurocrats will know the enormity of what they are doing. The bulldozer shovels will not merely be clearing ancient fences and stone walls: they will be burying the blood and the sweat and the hate and the love of a people with the oldest culture in the world, the first culture of the land.

I owe a word to the Healys, my father's family.

Their story belongs in another book and the picture of them which emerges from my mother's reported speech does them less than justice.

I lived with, and chafed at, my mother's denigration of the Healys and indeed made life harder for myself by challenging her. It was only much later that I came to understand that she was making what was an almost culturally-programmed response to them: her village was the best village, her family the best family and you did honour to it by denigrating the families or villages which threatened both.

137

There is no loss on the Healys. Most of them did well for themselves and their families. Typical was "that strap, Dotie" who produced a Franciscan priest, a university lecturer and like her sisters a clatter of nurses and teachers on a combination of a mechanic's salary and scholarship brains.

The fact was the Healy girls were all good-looking: they were great dancers and they had the pick of the men in their day and where they married, they married for love. My mother "married into the town" as they say, and married for love, too, if it goes to that but she could never forget the practicalities of a background in the culture of the land. The O'Donnells were always better than the Healys - until she lost her temper with one of the O'Donnells for a while.

When she died I wrote a piece about her in *The Western People.* Douglas Gageby called me from Dublin, on reading it, and urged me to sit down and expand it. "It will be better than anything you've written in your life" he said.

His persistence was such that he lured me to Sky Road in Clifden and in ten days we came away with a manuscript.

That was three years ago, well in advance of the "Roots" industry.

I should record my thanks to Aunt Agnes Healy for reading it and her observations on it from the Healy side; to Cousin Hubert McDermott, who is lecturing in English at University College, Galway: his criticism was as restrained as his father's praise but when Matt McDermott said: "You did very well" you had to be scoring 100 out of 100.

Evelyn, my wife, and daughter, Ann, had a lot to say about it and I hope in the end will like it.

Finally there was the happy accident that my second life-long friend in newspapers, Michael Finlan - more endearingly Mickey Finlan - forced my hand by giving the script to Desmond Kenny of Galway who was to publish the first edition.

If I am to add to the dedication it is to say this: I would hope it would stand as a tribute to all the smallholders of the West of Ireland whose story basically it is: if it gets their approval we will arrest the arrival of the Euro-bulldozers for another while.

Those last sentences were written in Achill in October 1978. The book was subsequently published and launched in Dublin by Charles J. Haughey, the present Taoiseach. It immediately entered the best-sellers' list and the edition sold out in a matter of months. Haughey himself was to become part of the story in the fight to keep the bulldozers of the Eurocrats at bay.

After the Papal visit to Knock Marian Shrine, the parish priest of Knock, Monsignor James Horan, started a campaign for an airport to serve Knock Shrine and the Connacht region. He was supported by prominent businessmen like Cathal Duffy of Castlebar, a director of the small local Castlebar airport. Duffy went on, with Monsignor Horan and businessmen from Sligo, Roscommon and Mayo, to form the board of Horan International.

Charles Haughey, as Taoiseach, sanctioned the building of the airport. It ran into the self-same political opposition as did the creation, by his father-in-law, Seán Lemass, of Shannon Airport over thirty years before. The grass and the rabbits, they said, would reclaim the runways. Shannon went on to become the world's first duty-free airport.

Horan International, in its first year of operation is the country's fastest growing airport and is serviced by Ryanair, Europe's fastest growing airline, which now operates scheduled services to London, Manchester and Birmingham. In the old days in Carracastle we would tell the time, working in the Bottom Meadow, from the passage of the red buses to and from Dublin. Today we can tell the time again by the Ryanair jets as they come in low to land four miles away at Horan International. The farm is on the flight path. There is a new and growing family on the hill and the house has been refurbished.

Ryanair is an independent airline which carries the rich promise for the entire region. In its first operating year it has achieved 85% seat occupancy on the British routes, the fruits of the bitter Irish diaspora of the 'Forties and 'Fifties when the young went eastwards to Birmingham, Manchester, Coventry and London or westwards to New York, Boston, Cleveland, Chicago or San Francisco.

The airport wasn't quite finished before the Jumbo jets brought the first US charter flights of the Irish home to land at Horan, tears of joy on their faces at being able to "land at our own airport at home". Some of those first American visitors elected to "walk home across the fields" they'd walked as children to pick morning mushrooms.

In the end our fight was not with the Eurocrats of Brussels but with the Dublin Establishment. Haughey's sanction for the airport came after James Horan had put together several smallholdings like Carracastle at a nominal price. These acres were as emotionally valuable to their owners as Carracastle was to my mother. That, more than the creation of the airport itself, was the great measure of Horan's gift of leadership.

Small wonder then when the new Government yielded to the Dublin knock-Knock campaign and abandoned the project, walking away from "the soggy, boggy, foggy" airport in the middle of nowhere – in which it had sunk £9.8 millions – James Horan rallied his Mayo neighbours at home and abroad to make a great meitheal to finish the airport at a cost of £3.2 millions.

James Horan used to tell us he was "an old man in a hurry". He saw the airport opened by Charles Haughey on a wet day, 30 May 1986. He welcomed the first jets from America. He led the first pilgrimage flight to Rome and promised to lead one to the great Marian Shrine at Lourdes.

I was there the morning he left. He was a failed giant of a man, tired now. He thanked everyone for making the day possible for him.

In Lourdes James Horan died in his sleep. Like my mother, he kept things at bay until his work was done. He returned to his airport and a funeral of national dimensions.

At Haughey's insistence the airport was renamed Horan International.

The growing success of Ryanair and its plans to expand further across the Atlantic ensures no grass will grow on the runway and the prosperity is spreading through the region. We will keep the bulldozers at bay for another while . . .

This second edition is a response to a popular demand created by the Radio Éireann programme "Booktime". It is produced by Mary Corcoran and the sensitive reading of Peadar Lambe resulted in a renewed demand for the book so long out of print. Lambe's interpretation and delivery deserves a better fate than a burial in some sound archive. Hopefully it will get it.

In the circumstances this edition catapults me into a new role as publisher. I have to thank my old colleague in journalism, Raymond Smith, for giving me, at one phone call, the full kit-book of advice and encouragement garnered by him over the last decade when he published his own best-selling series of books on politics and sport.

Brendan Kennelly, a kindred soul from the coast of Kerry and Professor of English at Dublin University, responded immediately and graciously to the invitation to write a Foreword to this present edition. I owe Brendan a double debt in that he has given me permission to reproduce his poetic tribute to my mother: it first appeared in *The Irish Times*.

Brendan Ellis and the staff of the Leinster Leader met a very tight deadline with superb professionalism. My daughter, Ann, designed the cover. Wonders were worked with the photos, most of which came from Kevin's collection. As always, Douglas Gageby will know how much of a role he has had in this edition as he has had in most things in my life in the past thirty years or more we have worked together.

Achill, June 1987